“Opera to me comes before everything else.”

- Wolfgang Amadeus Mozart

Mozart’s *DON GIOVANNI* is “the opera of all operas.”

- E. T. A. Hoffmann

Opera Journeys™ Mini Guide Series

Opera Classics Library™ Series

Opera Journeys™ Libretto Series

A History of Opera: Milestones and Metamorphoses

Opera Classics Library Puccini Companion: the Glorious Dozen

OVER 60 TITLES AVAILABLE:

•L'Africaine •Abduction from the Seraglio •Aida • Andrea Chénier
•The Barber of Seville •La Bohème •Boris Godunov • Carmen
•Cavalleria Rusticana • Così fan tutte •Der Freischütz •Der Rosenkavalier
•Die Fledermaus •Don Carlo •Don Giovanni •Don Pasquale •The Elixir of Love
•Elektra •Eugene Onegin •Exploring Wagner's Ring •Falstaff
•La Fanciulla del West •Faust •La Fille du Régiment •Fidelio
•The Flying Dutchman •Gianni Schicchi • Hansel and Gretel
•L'Italiana in Algeri •Julius Caesar •Lohengrin
•Lucia di Lammermoor •Macbeth • Madama Butterfly •The Magic Flute
•Manon •Manon Lescaut •The Marriage of Figaro •A Masked Ball
•The Mikado •Norma •Otello •I Pagliacci •Pelléas et Mélisande
•Porgy and Bess •The Rhinegold •Rigoletto •The Ring of the Nibelung
•La Rondine •Salome •Samson and Delilah •Siegfried •La Sonnambula
•Suor Angelica •Il Tabarro •The Tales of Hoffmann •Tannhäuser •Tosca
•La Traviata •Tristan and Isolde •Il Trittico •Il Trovatore •Turandot
•Twilight of the Gods •The Valkyrie •Werther •Wozzeck

All musical notations contained herein are original transcriptions by Opera Journeys Publishing.

Discography and Videography listings represent selections by the editors. Due to numerous re-issues of recordings and videos, issuer numbers and designations have been intentionally omitted.

WEB SITE: www.operajourneys.com E MAIL: operaj@bellsouth.net

Don Giovanni

Opera Classics Library™

Edited by Burton D. Fisher
Principal lecturer, *Opera Journeys Lecture Series*

Opera Journeys™ Publishing / Miami, Florida

Contents

a *Prelude........*
to OPERA CLASSICS LIBRARY's
Don Giovanni

The greatness of the opera art form lies in its inherent power to bring words to life through music: words can evoke thought; music can evoke feeling. Opera is a unique theatrical spectacle in which one can think and feel simultaneously.

Mozart's operas possess ingenious musical characterizations, his music brilliantly conveying and describing vital essences of the human personality and character. Two of his later operas stand out as hallmarks of that brilliant musical inventiveness: *The Marriage of Figaro* and *Don Giovanni.*

In *Don Giovanni,* Mozart assembled a brilliant cast: the opera seria characters of Donna Anna, Donna Elvira and Don Octavio, together with the opera buffa characters of Zerlina, Masetto, and of course Leporello. But it is Don Giovanni himself, who is the battlefield on which all the conflicts and tensions of these characters take place; Don Giovanni acts, and all the other characters react.

OPERA *CLASSICS LIBRARY* explores the magic of Mozart's *Don Giovanni.* The *Commentary and Analysis* section explores the genesis of the opera, particularly its inspiration from legends and classical literary works, plus insightful story and character analysis.

The text also contains a *Brief Story Synopsis, Principal Characters in Don Giovanni,* and *Story Narrative with Music Highlight Examples,* the latter containing original music transcriptions that are interspersed appropriately within the story's dramatic exposition. In addition, the text includes a *Discography, Videography,* and a *Dictionary of Opera and Musical Terms.*

The *Libretto* for *Don Giovanni* has been newly translated by the Opera Journeys staff with specific emphasis on retaining a literal translation, but also with the objective to provide a faithful translation that is easily comprehensible in modern and contemporary English; in this way, the substance of the drama becomes more intelligible. To enhance educational and study objectives, the *Libretto* also contains music highlight examples interspersed within the drama.

The opera art form is the sum of many artistic expressions: theatrical drama, music, scenery, poetry, dance, acting and gesture. In opera, it is the composer who is the dramatist, using the emotive power of his music to express intense, human conflicts. Opera's sublime fusion of words, music and all the theatrical arts provides powerful theater, an impact on one's sensibilities that can reach into the very depths of the human soul.

Don Giovanni is certainly a crown jewel of Mozart's many glorious operatic and musical inventions, but it remains a masterpiece of the lyric theater, a tribute to the art form as well as to its ingenious composer, and it is considered my many, "the opera of all operas."

Burton D. Fisher
Editor
OPERA CLASSICS LIBRARY

Don Giovanni

"Il Dissoluto Punito"

("Don Juan, The Rake Punished")

Dramma giocoso **("humorous drama")**

Opera in Italian in two acts

Music

by

Wolfgang Amadeus Mozart

Libretto by Lorenzo da Ponte

Premiere in Prague, 1787

Commentary and Analysis

Wolfgang Amadeus Mozart — 1756 to 1791— was born in Salzburg, Austria. His life-span was brief, but his phenomenal musical achievements have established him as one of the most important and inspired composers in Western history: music seemed to gush forth from his soul like fresh water from a spring. With his death at the age of thirty-five, one can only dream of the musical treasures that might have materialized from his music pen had he lived longer.

Along with Johann Sebastian Bach and Ludwig van Beethoven, Mozart is one of those three "immortals" of classical music. Superlatives about Mozart are inexhaustible: Tchaikovsky called him "the music Christ"; Haydn, a contemporary who revered and idolized him, claimed he was the best composer he ever knew; and Schubert wept over "the impressions of a brighter and better life he had imprinted on our souls." And Schumann wrote that there were some phenomena in the world about which words were ineffective to describe: much of Shakespeare, pages of Beethoven, and Mozart's last symphony, the forty-first.

Richard Wagner, who emphasized the power of the orchestra in his music dramas, assessed Mozart's symphonies: "He seemed to breathe into his instruments the passionate tones of the human voice....and thus raised the capacity of orchestral music for expressing the emotions to a height where it could represent the entire unsatisfied yearning of the heart."

Although Mozart's career was short, his musical output was tremendous by any standard: more than 600 works that include forty-one symphonies, twenty-seven piano concertos, more than thirty string quartets, many acclaimed quintets, world-famous violin and flute concertos, momentous piano and violin sonatas, and, of course, a legacy of sensational operas.

Mozart's father, Leopold, an eminent musician and composer in his own right, became the teacher and inspiration to his exceptionally talented and incredibly gifted prodigy child. The young Mozart brilliantly demonstrated a thorough command of the technical resources of musical composition: at age three he was able to play any tune he heard on the harpsichord; at age four he began composing his own music; at age six he gave his first public concert; by age twelve he had written ten symphonies, a cantata, and an opera; and at age thirteen he toured Italy, where in Rome, he astonished the music world by transcribing the full score of a complex religious composition after one hearing.

During the late eighteenth-century, a musician's livelihood depended solidly on patronage from the royalty and the aristocracy. Mozart and his sister, Nannerl, a skilled harpsichordist, frequently toured Europe together, performing at the courts in Austria, England, France, and Holland. But in his native Salzburg, Austria, the young Mozart felt artistically oppressed by the Archbishop. Eventually, he moved to Vienna where first-rate appointments and financial security emanated from the adoring support of both the Empress Maria Thèrése, and later her son, the Emperor Joseph II.

Opera legend tells the story of a post-performance meeting between Emperor Joseph II and Mozart in which the Emperor commented: "Too beautiful for our ears and too many notes, my dear Mozart." Mozart replied: "Exactly as many as necessary, Your Majesty."

Mozart said: "Opera to me comes before everything else." During the late eighteenth-century, opera genres consisted primarily of the Italian opera seria and opera buffa, and the German singspiel.

Opera seria defines the style of serious Italian operas whose subjects and themes dealt primarily with mythology, history, and Greek tragedy. In this genre, the music drama usually portrayed an heroic or tragic conflict that typically involved a moral dilemma, such as love vs. duty; essentially, these were tragic stories that usually resolved happily with due reward for rectitude, loyalty, and unselfishness.

Opera buffa was an Italian genre of comic opera, that, like its predecessor, the commedia dell'arte, presented satire and parodies about real-life situations. The commedia dell'arte was a theatrical tradition that evolved during the Renaissance and had been performed by troupes of strolling players; their satire and irony would ridicule every aspect of their society and its institutions through the characterization of humorous or hypocritical situations involving cunning servants, scheming doctors, and duped masters.

In Mozart's time, opera buffa was perhaps the most popular operatic form, its life continuing well into the nineteenth century in the hands of the Italian masters: Rossini and Donizetti. German singspiel, similar to Italian opera buffa, was specifically comic opera, but with spoken dialogue rather than accompanied recitative between its musical numbers.

Social upheavals and ideological transitions were brewing in Mozart's time. The Enlightenment dominated the eighteenth century, ultimately inspiring the American and French Revolutions, significant turning points of western history that would overturn centuries of social injustice. Mozart relished the opportunity to portray themes in his operas in which the common man struggled for his rights against the tyranny and oppression of his aristocratic masters. Opera buffa provided a convenient theatrical vehicle in which the ideals of democracy could be expressed in art. Whereas the aristocracy identified and became flattered by the exalted personalities, gods, and heroes portrayed in the pretentious pomp and formality of the opera seria, the satire and humor of opera buffa, provided an arena to express the frustrations of social injustices suffered by the lower classes of society. In particular, Mozart's opera buffa, *The Marriage of Figaro*, portrays servants more clever than their selfish, unscrupulous, and arrogant masters. Napoleon would later conclude that *The Marriage of Figaro*, both the Mozart opera and its source Beaumarchais play, was the "Revolution in action."

Mozart wrote over eighteen operas, among them: *Bastien and Bastienne* (1768); *La Finta Semplice* (1768); *Mitridate, Rè di Ponto* (1770); *Ascanio in Alba* (1771); *Il Sogno di Scipione* (1772); *Lucio Silla* (1772); *La Finta Giardiniera* (1774); *Idomeneo, Rè di Creta* (1781); *Die Entführung aus dem Serail* ("The Abduction from the Seraglio") (1782); *Der Schauspieldirektor* (1786); *Le Nozze di Figaro*, ("The Marriage of Figaro") (1786); *Don Giovanni* (1787); *Così fan tutte* (1790); *Die Zauberflöte* ("The Magic Flute") (1791); and *La Clemenza di Tito* (1791).

During Mozart's time — the second half of the eighteenth century — the Italians set the international standards for opera: Italian was the universal language of music and opera, and Italian opera was what Mozart's Austrian audiences and most of the rest of Europe wanted most. Therefore, even though Mozart was an Austrian, his country part of the Holy Roman Empire, most of Mozart's operas were written to Italian librettos.

Mozart's most popular Italian operas are: *The Marriage of Figaro* ("Le Nozze di Figaro"), an opera buffa that represented his first collaboration with his most famous librettist, Lorenzo da Ponte; *Don Giovanni*, technically an opera buffa but designated a "dramma giocoso" ("humorous drama" or "playful play"), that is essentially a combination of both the opera buffa and opera seria genres; *Così fan tutte* ("Thus do all women behave"), another blend of the opera seria with the opera buffa; and his last opera, *La Clemenza di Tito* ("The Clemency of Titus"), an opera seria commissioned to celebrate the coronation in Prague of the Emperor Leopold II as King of Bohemia. Nevertheless, Italians have historically shunned Mozart's Italian operas, claiming they were not "Italian" enough; a La Scala production of a Mozart Italian opera is a rare event. Mozart's most popular German operas are: *Die Zauberflöte* ("The Magic Flute"), and *Die Entführung aus dem Serail* ("The Abduction from the Seraglio."), both operas stylistically singspiel works.

Mozart's operas receive the same extravagant praise as his instrumental music, his musical characterizations considered to capture a sublime unity of both the smiles and tears of life. To some, *Don Giovanni* is the finest opera ever written; some prefer *The Magic Flute*; and still others choose *The Marriage of Figaro,* and nothing could be more praiseworthy of Mozart's genius than the musicologist William Mann's conclusion that *Così fan tutte* contains "the most captivating music ever composed."

So Mozart addicts continue to argue vociferously about which is his best opera: *Così fan tutte*, considered by some to be his most exquisite, sophisticated, and subtle work; *The Marriage of Figaro*, sometimes called the perfect opera buffa, and his most inspired because of the comic effectiveness of its political and social implications; or *Don Giovanni,* because of its alternation of the light and comic with the darker overtones of genuine tragedy. In the end, it is a better or best argument, but one in which artistic greatness remains patent and acknowledged.

Mozart was unequivocal about his opera objectives: "In an opera, poetry must be altogether the obedient daughter of the music." Nevertheless, he indeed took great care in selecting that poetry, relentlessly admonishing his librettists to produce words that he could illuminate and transcend with his music. To an opera composer of such incredible genius as Mozart, words performed through music expressed what language alone had exhausted.

Musically, Mozart's works epitomize the Classical style of the late eighteenth-century, the goal of which was to conform to specific standards and forms, to be succinct, clear, well balanced, but at the same time, develop musical ideas to a heightened emotional fullness. Although Mozart was a quintessential Classicist, much of the greatness of his music emanates from his ingenious combination of the Italian inclination for graceful melody with a German proclivity for formality and contrapuntal perfection.

Mozart is considered the consummate master of translating "dramatic truth" into his music: that is the vital element in his musical language; an ingenious portrayal of complex human emotions, passions, and feelings. Opera, or music drama, by its very nature, is essentially an art form concerned with the emotions and behavior of human beings, so the success of an opera lies in its ability to convey a realistic panorama of human character through its music. Mozart understood his fellow human beings, and ingeniously translated that insight through his musical language.

Mozart's ingenious ability to bare the soul of his characters was almost Shakespearean: his musical characterizations are truthful representations of universal humanity that express human virtues, aspirations, inconsistencies, peculiarities, flaws and foibles. But Mozart usually bares the truth and rarely suggests any puritanical judgment or moralization of his characters' behavior and actions, prompting Beethoven to lament that in *Don Giovanni* and *The Marriage of Figaro*, Mozart had squandered his genius on immoral and licentious subjects.

Nevertheless, that spotlight on the individual makes Mozart a bridge between eighteenth and nineteenth century operas. Before him, in the opera seria genre, operas portrayed abstract emotion. But Mozart was anticipating the transition to the Romantic movement that was to begin soon after his death. As such, Mozart's characterizations made opera come alive; he endowed his characters with definite and distinctive musical personalities, all possessing profound sentiments and feelings.

In earlier works, like Gluck's opera serias, the dramatic form would imitate the style of the Greek theater: an individual's passions and the dramatic situations would generally transfer to the chorus for narration, commentary, or summation. Mozart clearly perceived the vast possibilities of the operatic form as a means of musically creating characterization: in his operas, great and small characters move, think and breathe on the human level; therefore, Mozart's characters discard the masks of Greek drama and appear as individuals with recognizable personalities. Mozart innovated the use of ensembles to capture the interaction between characters; his ensembles are almost symphonic in grandeur, moments in which each individual character's emotions, passions, feelings, and reactions stand out in high relief.

Mozart's musical characterization are extraordinary and insightful, ingenious portrayals of real and complex humanity in their conduct and character. As a consequence, audiences have been enthralled for over two-hundred years with his characterizations: *Don Giovanni*'s Donna Anna, Donna Elvira, Zerlina, Masetto, Leporello, and Don Giovanni himself; *The Marriage of Figaro*'s Count and Countess Almaviva, Cherubino, Dr. Bartolo, Marcellina, Susanna, and Figaro. All of these Mozart characters are profoundly human: they act with passion, yet they are portrayed musically with those special Mozartian qualities of dignity and sentiment.

In the end, like Shakespeare, Mozart's characterizations have become timeless representations of humanity. His opera characterizations are as contemporary in the twentieth century as they were in the late eighteenth century, even though costumes and customs may have changed. So Count Almaviva, in *The Marriage of Figaro*, attempting to exercise his feudal right of droit du seigneur, may be no different than a wealthy twentieth-century chief executive living in his Connecticut mansion, legally forbidden — but desiring — to bed his illegal alien housekeeper against her wishes. Art achieves greatness by portraying truths, its true greatness its ability to absorb its listener, consciously or subconsciously. In that sense, art is indeed a mirror of the self.

To achieve those spectacular results in musical characterization, Mozart became a magician in developing and using various techniques of his musical language to portray and communicate human passions: envy, revenge, or noble love. He expressed those qualities through distinguishing melody, through rhythm, tempo, pitch, and through accent and speech inflection.

But perhaps more importantly, Mozart excelled in using the specific qualities of certain key signatures for special effects: often G major is the key for rustic life and the common people; D minor, appearing solemnly in the Overture and final scene of *Don Giovanni,* is his key for Sturm und Drang, (storm and stress); and A major, the seductive key for sensuous love scenes. When characters are in trouble, they sing in keys far removed from the home key: as they get out of trouble, they return to that key, reducing the tension.

Mozart's theatrical genius was his ability to express truly human qualities in his music. He endowed his character creations with a universal and sublime uniqueness, and in the end, created an unchallenged immortality for both composer and his operatic achievements.

The Marriage of Figaro, Don Giovanni, and *Così fan tutte*, were composed during the social and political upheavals of the late eighteenth century. This trilogy of operas, all with librettos written by Lorenzo da Ponte, deal satirically with despicable aspects of human character, whose transformation was the very focus of the Enlightenment idealism that precipitated the French Revolution.

The engines that drive the plots of *The Marriage of Figaro* and *Don Giovanni* are the moral foibles and peccadilloes of aristocratic men: in particular, Count Almaviva and Don Giovanni are nobles who can almost be perceived by modern standards as criminals; they are unstable, wildly libidinous, and consider themselves above the law. Similarly, in *Così fan tutte*, the actions of the women can be perceived as transcending moral law, not to mention some of the inhumane actions of the men.

The themes of all three works are concerned with seduction, seduction that invariably ends in hapless failure. On Mozart's stage, these flawed individuals stand in the center of a symbolic ideological bridge between the eighteenth century Enlightenment and nineteenth century Romanticism. As such, their despicable actions represent a subtle forecast to the forthcoming social upheavals, the great ideological transition in Western history that ended the ancien régime.

But in Mozart's *Don Giovanni* and *The Marriage of Figaro*, social classes collide on the stage with sentiment and insight: Mozart's musical characterizations range in his operas from underdogs to demigods, but when he deals with peasants and the lower classes, he is subtle, compassionate and loving. So Mozart's heroes become those bright characters who occupy the lower stations, those Figaros, Susannas, Zerlinas and Masettos, victims of social injustices whom he ennobles with poignant musical portrayals of their complex personal emotion, sensitivity, hope, sadness, envy, passion, revenge, and their love and compassion.

The commission for *Don Giovanni* followed the triumphant productions of *The Marriage of Figaro* in both Vienna and Prague in 1786. Although those "Don Juan" plays, which had derived from legends were considered by the aristocracy to have descended to the level of vulgarity, Prague was not directly under the control of the imperial Hapsburgs; therefore, the censorship and restriction of underlying elements of its story was limited, if nonexistent.

For *Don Giovanni,* Mozart again chose as his librettist that peripatetic scholar and entrepreneur, Lorenzo da Ponte, the man who had earlier supplied the text for *The Marriage of Figaro* (and later *Così fan tutte*). Da Ponte was a close friend of the notorious Casanova de Seingalt, reputedly his assistant for selected sections of the *Don Giovanni* libretto.

Da Ponte was born in Italy in 1749, and died in America in 1838. He was born Emmanuel Conegliano, converted from Judaism, and was later baptized, taking the name da Ponte in honor of the Bishop of Ceneda. Da Ponte would take holy orders in 1773, but he quickly tired of the languor of seminary life: he described his subsequent picaresque life in his biography, which bears an uncanny resemblance to that of his libertine romantic hero, Don Giovanni.

Da Ponte was always involved in scandals and intrigues, forcing him to be banished from Venice, and later leave England under threat of imprisonment for financial difficulties. In 1805, he emigrated to the United States, taught Italian at Columbia University, and is credited with having introduced the Italian classics to America. He later became an opera impresario; in 1825, he may have been the first to present Italian opera in the United States.

In da Ponte's self-serving *Extract from the Life of Lorenzo Da Ponte* (1819), he ennobles himself in his explanation as to why Mozart chose him as his inspirational poet: "Because Mozart knew very well that the success of an opera depends, first of all, on the poet.....that a composer, who is, in regard to drama, what a painter is in regard to colors, can never do without effect, unless excited and animated by the words of a poet, whose province is to choose a subject susceptible of variety, movement, and action, to prepare, to suspend, to bring about the catastrophe, to exhibit characters interesting, comic, well supported, and calculated for stage effect, to write his recitative short, but substantial, his airs various, new, and well situated; and his fine verses easy, harmonious, and almost singing of themselves....."

Certainly, in da Ponte's librettos for Mozart operas, he indeed ascribed religiously to those literary and dramatic disciplines and qualities he so eloquently congratulated himself for in his autobiography.

Goethe testified to the popularity and drawing power of the "Don Juan" stories among the common people, after he witnessed an opera on the subject in Rome in 1787: "There could not have been a soul alive (in Rome, right down to the greengrocer and his children) who had not seen Don Juan roasting in Hell, and the Commendatore, as a blessed spirit, ascending to Heaven."

Don Juan legends and myths trace their genesis, like the Faust story, to the exploits of a personage who actually lived. The tale describes Don Juan, a member of the noble Tenorio family, who in the fourteenth century, is reputed to have been a perpetrator of plots against the entire female population of Seville.

The first play to reach the stage was by the Spanish dramatist, Gabriel Tellez (1584-1648), who wrote under the pseudonym Tirso de Molina: *El Burlador de Sevilla y Convivado de Piedra* ("The Rake of Seville and the Stone Guest.") In the play's finale, Don Juan brazenly invites the Stone Guest to dine with him, and to his consternation, the statue accepts. They dine in a nearby chapel: the dishes at their supper contain scorpions and snakes, the wine is gall and verjuice, and the dinner music is a penitential psalm. Then the statue vanishes, at which time Don Juan is consigned to Hell.

Other inspirations for the da Ponte/Mozart story were Molière's *Le Festin de Pierre* (1665) ("The Feast of Stone"), Righini's *Il Convitato di Pietra ossia Il Dissoluto punito* (1776), the German comedy (comödie) *Das steinerne Gastmahl* (1760), and Gluck's pantomime ballet *Don Juan, ou Le Festin de Pierre* (1761). Molière's play, in particular, aroused great controversy owing to the religious and social elements he portrayed: Don Juan's atheism and lack of gallantry toward the poor was deemed to be un-Catholic and un-Spanish, not to mention his sins of rape and seduction.

The eighteenth-century plays of the very popular Carlo Goldoni were noted for their wit and skill in satirizing social pretension. Goldoni treated the subject in his play, *Don Giovanni Tenorio, o sia Il Dissoluto* (1736), his particular innovations that Donna Anna was betrothed to Don Octavio against her will, and his introduction of Donna Elvira, the presumably mad woman who continuously interferes with Don Juan's seductive adventures. However, Da Ponte's basic framework for his libretto for Mozart's opera was Bertati's contemporary one-act opera, *Don Giovanni, or sia il Convitato di Pietra* (1787), musically scored by Giuseppe Gazzaniga, a highly prolific and esteemed opera composer of the late eighteenth century.

From their very beginnings, Don Juan stories about the libertine rake of legend were extremely popular medieval morality plays, certainly during the God-centered Middle Ages when society literally lived between hell and damnation. The stories became a popular vehicle for strolling puppet theaters, whose audiences relished its underlying allegorical struggle between the forces of good and evil, and the ultimate punishment of the classic transgressor.

In these stories, Don Juan is a rebel against conventional morality, a dissolute sinner, and a promiscuous, treacherous, and murderous man; by the demands of a morality play, he must receive divine justice through punishment. Like all humanity, Don Juan is a fatally flawed character, yet he is a compellingly fascinating and commanding figure. Nevertheless, he is a menace and danger to society, particularly in his attractiveness to weak and vulnerable women: three of those women appear in high-relief in the Mozart/da Ponte version of the story: Donna Anna, Donna Elvira and Zerlina. In the Mozart opera, each woman has her own particular obsession and fascination with Don Giovanni; each is aware of his evil, but each is ready and willing to surrender to him.

Mozart's Don Giovanni boldly confronts his world, a Faust committing the sin of curiosity, or a Carmen obsessed with her freedom to love whom she wants. However, Don Giovanni can be viewed as an archetype of every man or woman's alter ego, a man who faces that eternal conflict of the tension, desire and craving for love, and the struggle between emotion and reason, the spirit and the flesh, or the sacred and the profane. Don Giovanni represents powerful and uncontrollable irrational forces of humanity, an ambivalent and paradoxical world, in which he can either be viewed as a blessing or a curse.

George Bernard Shaw's *Man and Superman,* interprets Don Giovanni as the incarnation of an evolutionary "life force," its hero, a demonic and satanic force of evil that rises to challenge God himself.

Throughout its two hundred year plus history, many have considered Mozart's *Don Giovanni* "the opera of all operas," possibly the most perfect opera ever composed. It is a monumental wonder of musical imagination, a work containing towering music with unrivalled beauty, and a plot whose dramatic essence contains timeless themes; perhaps a more appropriate accolade attributable to this immortal masterpiece would be "THE opera of the second millennium."

During the late eighteenth century, opera buffa was the most popular opera genre, but at the same time, the opera seria genre was en route to obsolescence. Mozart largely modeled *Don Giovanni* on the style of *The Marriage of Figaro,* a synthesis of the opera buffa comic style with the seriousness of the opera seria. Although da Ponte wanted his scenario to be entirely comedic — a satire in the old classic tradition — Mozart perceived an inner depth in the story and was determined to inject seriousness into the plot.

The designation "dramma" in Mozart's time signified the grander, heroic world of opera seria, while "giocoso" denoted "gaiety" or "frolic." *Don Giovanni* was designated a "dramma giocoso," a "humorous drama," and therefore represents the compromise between composer and librettist, the resulting work containing a profound seriousness melded with riotous comedy and humor. Mozart himself would at times casually refer to the opera as an opera buffa.

But *Don Giovanni* is essentially a tragicomedy, in which boisterous laughter becomes fused with serious tears, where slapstick, farcical comedy, and humor fuse with the supernatural might of avenging providence. The blending of all of these elements, in many respects, heightens the poignancy and eeriness of the tragedy.

To heighten the effect of tragicomedy, like *The Marriage of Figaro* and the later *Così fan tutte*, the plot continuously alternates between comedy and satire, and then quickly plunges into the darker shades of genuine tragedy: Donna Anna is a genuine opera seria personality, a woman of driving passions, who portrays profound grief for her father's death, and a relentless obsession for revenge against Don Giovanni.

Donna Elvira is also essentially an opera seria character, a spurned woman who alternates between love, compassion, and revenge. Likewise, Don Octavio's noble devotion and outpourings of love for Donna Anna are sentiments so typical of the opera seria genre. And nothing could be more derivative of the opera seria than the forces of supernatural retribution, the Commandant coming to life to lead Don Giovanni to his ultimate doom and eternal punishment.

But the smiles, sublime humor, and the gaiety of opera buffa are dutifully portrayed in the playful quarrels and reconciliations of Masetto and Zerlina, and the Don's thrashing of Masetto. However, Leporello is the true opera buffa character: his wit and humor in the Catalogue aria, his pleasure in imitating his master's escapades, and his admonishments to his master to change his dissolute life-style.

Don Giovanni is a man with a romantic compulsion, a cold and insensitive adventurer living a tension between desire and fulfillment. The profligate Don Giovanni is governed by a single motivation: his flaunting of society and its rules in the pursuit of sexual pleasure and conquest.

Leporello ironically tells Donna Elvira about his master's compulsions in the Catalogue aria, a moment of laughter, yet a moment of tears for the vanquished: "He conquers the old ones for the pleasure of adding them to the list. But his predominant passion is the young beginner. He doesn't mind if she's rich, or ugly, or beautiful. You know what he does, providing she wears a skirt."

Don Giovanni is an escapading antihero, an adventurer whose charismatic personality captivates and overwhelms all who encounter him: his victims remain in awe or shock, yet his demonic engine continues to grind steadily with a passionate ebullience and a forceful vitality.

In our times, the classic Don Juan legends have passed from the realm of theater into Freudian interpretation: the psychiatric language speaks about the "Don Juan" complex, in which, the hero fails to recognize his true self-hiding behind his mask; there is a cold heart behind his masquerade of obsessive sexuality and amorous passion.

Modern psychologists cite that Don Giovanni's adventures hide an unconscious male fantasy; that obsession for blissful union — or reunion — with his mother. As such, his unconscious obsessions have driven him into sexual adventures that are not the outcome of real feelings, but rather, illusory obsessions with sex and conquest that are the chronic symptoms of a disease that is incomprehensible to him.

In that context, Don Giovanni is never capable of experiencing true love, because he has erected a subconscious defense, a fear that overshadows his narcissistic selfishness and even selflessness. In effect, Don Giovanni is continually defending himself against the threat of women, impetuously chasing his next conquest as he escapes in desperation from the last.

So behind that facade of the swashbuckling, boudoir-hopping, serial sexist, lurks a perpetual adolescent seeking instant gratification; or perhaps a latent homosexual actually hating women; or perhaps an antihero intent on evil who slays an interfering father (the Commandant). In that context, Don Giovanni is in pursuit of one unsatisfactory mother-image after another. To stretch the psychological thesis even further, it has even been suggested that Don Giovanni himself is an incarnation of a fertility god, so to attend a Don Giovanni performance is to participate in the celebration of some kind of mythic fertility ritual.

But in spite of modern psychological interpretations, *Don Giovanni* is first and foremost a classical morality play: as such, good must conquer evil. Don Giovanni cannot flaunt society's norms with his carefree pursuit of sexual pleasure, so ultimately, he must receive divine retribution and punishment; it becomes the man he murdered, the Commandant, who appears to him as a metaphysical apparition, the embodiment of divine law, destiny, and the moral voice of righteousness. In the end, Don Giovanni's ultimate fate is horrible and gruesome, yet in the context of a morality play he must be punished; it is Mozart's genius that elevates Don Giovanni's demise to an incomparable sublimity.

Don Giovanni is the central catalyst of the drama who evokes all of the responses and actions from the other characters; when Don Giovanni acts, everyone else reacts. He is an almost opaque hero who becomes defined by those he pursues.

Yet as Don Giovanni pursues his picaresque adventures, the inner soul of the hero is concealed; there are no lengthy Wagnerian-style introspective narrations in which Don Giovanni reveals the deep inner workings of his soul. Yet, he instinctively and intuitively knows his surrounding world and senses the vulnerability of the characters that confront him: he will exploit all of them, and all of them will be humbled and humiliated; in the process, each one will become aware of his own weaknesses and vulnerabilities.

The three principal female characters in this drama — Donna Anna, Donna Elvira and Zerlina — yearn and crave for love, and in that pursuit they experience anxiety and pain. Mozart and da Ponte shift the wages of sin from sinner to the sinned against. In defending their failures, they all find a way to blame Don Giovanni for their dilemma, and at times, they accuse each other of cruelty. But in truth, it is Don Giovanni who is cruel; it is Don Giovanni who is steadfast and resolute in his heartless and callous pursuits, and in the end, the pursued stand dumbfounded and in wonder and awe. Mozart's music ingeniously weaves together these individual personalities, breathing life into their agonies and their ecstasies; their heartbeats pound with emotional gravitas, and their feelings and anxieties are sometimes comic and sometimes serious — and sometimes both.

In *Don Giovanni*'s three female characters, the diverse spectrum of womanhood is rendered complete: the great opera seria character of the avenging Donna Anna, the sentimental and spurned Donna Elvira, and the crafty but sympathetic peasant girl Zerlina.

Donna Anna's character shades the opera with both darkness and romanticism, and it is Donna Anna's grief in her father's death and murder that is a mainspring of the drama. Mozart places total humanity in Donna Anna, the daughter of an aristocratic nobleman, and a woman who becomes completely consumed by her passion for revenge — and love.

It is never quite clear whether Donna Anna was indeed seduced and raped by Don Giovanni, or if she was a willing participant in a clandestine liaison with him. It is a most dramatic episode when Donna Anna tells Don Octavio that through his voice and manner, she recognizes Don Giovanni as her father's murderer and her assailant from the night before. To Mozart's eighteenth century audience, Donna Anna had certainly invited Don Giovanni to her apartment that night, for there are noticeable gaps and discrepancies in her story. Specifically, her explanation to Don Octavio — her fiance — is far too concerned with the presumed attack on her honor, and hardly concerned with the killing of her father.

Don Giovanni made his conquest and decided to leave, a man of the chase and the kill who had no concern for the carcass after the conquest. It has been speculated that Donna Anna was indeed seduced, and willingly welcomed their amorous episode, but like all of his conquests, when it was over, it was over. So Donna Anna's revenge against Don Giovanni as the murderer of her father stands as a subterfuge for her more extreme passion: her revenge against a perfidious lover.

Mozart's supreme devotee, Ernst Theodor Amadeus Hoffmann, an early nineteenth-century German Romantic writer whose obsession with Mozart and his opera *Don Giovanni* compelled him to change his third name from Wilhelm to Amadeus, hypothesized Donna Anna's true motivations in one of his fantastic tales: *Don Juan* (1813), republished as *Phantasiestucke in Callots Manier* (1814).

Hoffmann concluded that Donna Anna was a "divine woman over whose pure spirit, evil is powerless." Yet, Hoffmann concluded that Donna Anna was a profoundly sensuous woman who was secretly aflame with desire for Don Giovanni; it is her impassioned call for revenge against Don Giovanni for violating her honor, "Or sai chi l'onore," in which Hoffmann suggests that Donna Anna had been willingly seduced by Don Giovanni, and was deeply in love with him.

The unfortunate corollary to Hoffmann's elevation of Donna Anna is that in his fantastic tale he portrays Donna Elvira as a caricature, a less voluptuous and more unworthy example of womanhood than Donna Anna. Hoffmann portrays her as the "tall, emaciated Donna Elvira, bearing visible signs of great, but faded beauty." Da Ponte's libretto specifies only that she be young, and in a later tribute, Baudelaire refers to her as "the chaste and thin Elvira."

Donna Elvira was the specific creation of Molière's version of the legend in his *Le Festin de Pierre* (1665), in which, Elvira became a strong-minded woman with a complex and multidimensional personality, perhaps possessing the most profound feelings of all the female characters. Mozart's musical portrait of Donna Elvira provides a delicate balance between sympathy and rage; she is a spurned and humiliated woman who is constantly tormented and degraded. Yet, Donna Elvira brings to the fore the paradoxes of how quickly love or hate can be triggered: she becomes obsessed with vengeance, but at the same time, she is ever doting and willingly available as an easy conquest for Don Giovanni — if he promises to return to her and mend his ways.

Donna Elvira represents a magnificent portrait of an archetypal spurned woman: she was a former nun who was seduced by Don Giovanni while she was in a convent, and the memory of that experience has transformed into her life's obsession; she is determined to tear out Don Giovanni's heart unless he returns to her. But Donna Elvira is the only woman in the story who openly expresses true fidelity to Don Giovanni, and in that sense, she represents the real threat to his defenses, perhaps the reason he fights her off so cruelly. (Da Ponte even suggests that Don Giovanni married her because it was the only way he could control her.)

Donna Elvira pursues Don Giovanni with an impassioned single-mindedness, her love for him not just merely a passing episode, but a decisive passion. In that sense, Donna Elvira, of all the women in the opera, is the one character whose entire human essence parallels that of Don Giovanni. Like Don Giovanni, she is constantly in pursuit of the ideal, craving and yearning for love. It was Don Giovanni who kindled a spark in Elvira, and she shares that same consuming passion for love that burns within him.

Donna Elvira's "Ah! Fuggi il tradito" has a passionate and fiery fury, cries that reveal the torment in her soul. But her final outburst of revenge and hatred against Don Giovanni merely reconfirm the proximity of the passions of love and hate. Nevertheless, Donna Elvira is determined to win back Don Giovanni's love, even after she recognizes the hopelessness of her quest.

Donna Elvira's misfortune was that her apparently first and only love experience became none other than the licentious Don Giovanni. It was obviously a euphoric moment for her, and its memory has caused her to surrender her soul, her life, her love, and her future to a man she refuses to abandon. Donna Elvira, like Donna Anna, is a tragic and tormented personality. She thirsts for tenderness, but passes from outrage and indignation to powerless defeat and despair. In the end, she realizes that her dreams are all illusions, and she will only find solace in her memories.

Don Octavio is the great comforter and consoler of Donna Anna, her husband-to-be. He is a man of admirable sentiments, constantly joining his beloved Donna Anna in sharing her suffering, and solemnly offering her solace by supporting her need for revenge.

When Donna Anna recognizes that Don Giovanni was her seducer and the murderer of her father, Don Octavio listens in shock. At first he offers appropriate sympathy, but then responds incredulously; he never heard of a cavalier capable of so black a crime, and swears that it is his duty as Donna Anna's lover and friend to vindicate her honor.

Essentially, Don Octavio is colorless and docile, yet he is worthy and well-meaning, at times though, appearing to be a dutiful and obedient parasite of desirable and voluptuous women. He seems indecisive, taking quite a long time to reach his conclusion that Don Giovanni is indeed the villain, but he of course does not know that Donna Anna has reached her conclusions through first hand experience. Somehow, Don Octavio alleges Don Giovanni's guilt based on his unsuccessful attempt to seduce Zerlina, and his later thrashing of Masetto. But none of Don Octavio's conclusions would pass the test of the smoking gun. Essentially, Don Octavio, the man who is in love with Donna Anna, cannot face the truth that his beloved had been dishonored by another man, no less the notorious Don Giovanni.

Zerlina is ambivalent: she is either an innocent country girl, or a saucy, wily, and ever-so-omniscient flirt; Mozart's music for her is always full of a sense of guile and trickery.

When Don Giovanni serenades Zerlina in lieu of seducing her, "Là ci darem la mano," Mozart's music dissolves any animosity that she might bear toward Don Giovanni, the music magically contrasting Don Giovanni's aristocratic bearing against Zerlina's country-girl shyness and presumed innocence. But the serenade is a masterly instance of Don Giovanni's insincerity, and Zerlina is placed in conflict between emotion and reason; at certain moments she actually believes — or wants to believe — his expansive talk, and that an amorous liaison with an aristocrat will elevate her on the social ladder. Mozart's cynical eighteenth century audience certainly laughed at Zerlina's presumed innocence and gullibility, but they had more pleasure in anticipating the villain's defeat.

"Là ci darem la mano" is a wonderfully sensuous and exquisite musical number: it is begun by Don Giovanni, and then builds to a duet with Zerlina; it is Don Giovanni's invitation to Zerlina to escape with him to the little house where they will be married — or pretend to be married. Both Don Giovanni and Zerlina seem to be irresistible to each other; both display subtle explosions of physical attraction, chemistry, true desire and a harmony of their souls. Zerlina vacillates with indecision. She wants to, and doesn't want to, but then feels herself weakening: their "Andiam" that concludes the duet, conveys a sense of sublime excitement and pleasure.

Later, Zerlina uses her irresistible charm to console Masetto after his thrashing by Don Giovanni, exploiting his exaggeration of his injuries with irresistible arguments: love will resolve everything. Zerlina's "Batti, batti o mio Masetto" is a light and lovely moment of supreme opera buffa, but it nevertheless expresses true sentiment and love.

The character of Leporello is a direct descendant of the commedia dell'arte tradition. He is that classic satirical opera buffa character, the comic servant who expresses mock anxieties and rebellious indignation when he complains sarcastically and bitterly about the conditions of his employment for his libertine master — irregular meals, lack of sleep, and endless vigils waiting for his master in wind and rain: "Notte e giorno faticar." Although he is cynical when he congratulates Don Giovanni on his success at seducing a daughter and at the same time eliminating the father, he is horrified by the death of the Commandant, an "eccesso" ("excess") that was seemingly provoked, but certainly the last thing he or Don Giovanni ever intended.

Leporello expresses sincere compassion for Donna Elvira when he tries to persuade her — through the Catalogue — of his master's unworthiness; that she is not the first nor the last of his master's conquests, but of course he unhesitatingly describes his master's preferences and adventures with obvious pride. And in true opera buffa tradition, Leporello becomes the unwitting victim of Don Giovanni's excesses on two occasions: in the Act I finale when he becomes the accused seducer of Zerlina, and in his pitiful predicament when he is caught by Don Giovanni's avengers in Act II.

Although Leporello expresses righteous indignation toward Don Giovanni when he condemns his master's profligate life and threatens to leave his service, his loyalty quickly returns after Don Giovanni's bonus compensation.

Leporello relishes his moments as a Don Giovanni-in-training; imitation is indeed the greatest form of flattery. When Leporello is among the peasants, he imitates his master's habits and mannerisms, hopeful that among so many young women there might be a conquest for him too. And although it is an exaggerated moment, he obviously enjoys the charade and impersonation of his master when he woos Donna Elvira: "Son per voi tutta foco" ("I'm all aflame for you.")

The Leporello character is a magnificent blend of wit, comedy and seriousness: a quintessential opera buffa character.

At the conclusion of Act I, the entrance of the three masked characters provides a magnificent moment for ambivalent meanings. The three masked characters — Donna Anna, Donna Elvira, and Don Octavio — arrive at Don Giovanni's festivities, the music and text exploding with the strains of "Viva la libertà." (For obvious reasons, da Ponte intentionally withheld this portion of the opera text when he submitted it to the censors.)

For each character, liberty may have a different meaning: for Don Giovanni himself, liberty is perhaps his right to exploit his surrounding world, a goal that he has accomplished by inducing everyone to his castle, if only for the opportunity to seduce Zerlina; for Leporello, liberty could define his freedom to emulate the licentious actions of his master; for Zerlina, liberty could mean a higher social status if she spends a night with the aristocratic Don Giovanni, an idea she disingenuously revealed earlier during the "Là ci darem la mano" duet; and for Masetto, liberty could mean his right to fight against the social injustices to which he has become a victim.

And for those three masked characters, liberty is their freedom to enter Don Giovanni's iniquitous world and unmask, expose, and punish the profligate seducer and evil murderer.

The banquet scene of *Don Giovanni* is a great tour-de-force of lyric theater, a magnificent blend of comedy and tragedy. Donna Elvira had again been pleading with Don Giovanni to mend his ways and return to her love nest, but she was unsuccessful. As she leaves in anguish and torment, she turns to panic when she sees the Statue (the Commandant), arriving to dine with Don Giovanni. Leporello is overcome with fear and terror and hides under the table. But Don Giovanni confronts the Statue with ferocious courage, a symbolic moment when time stops and he is forced to look inward.

When Don Giovanni grasps the Statue, he feels an unmistakable coldness, perhaps the inhuman coldness lurking within his own inner soul. He cannot free himself from the grasp of the Statue, even as flames begin to engulf him. Nevertheless, Don Giovanni is heedless to the Statue's commands; he remains resolute and will not change his ways or repent for his dissolute life.

Mozart inventively scored this chilling and frightening moment in the dark and mysterious key of D minor, the music recalling the Overture and the death of the Commandant in Act I; it is a brilliant musical portrait of that defining moment in which the universal sinner is about to receive divine retribution for his transgressions.

Don Giovanni is doomed to Hell by fire, a transformation that will expurgate his soul, and the means by which he can be resurrected with new insight, understanding, awareness and compassion. In order for Don Giovanni to replace his inhumanity with true love and compassion, he must repent. But he courageously refuses, and avenging devils drag the unrepentant sinner to eternal punishment.

Don Giovanni represented archetypal evil: he was cruel, seductive, coarse and arrogant. But Don Giovanni's demise was heroic; even though he may have sensed his irrevocable damnation, he was unequivocally courageous and resolute in his refusal to repent, intransigent to change and become anything other than his reprobate self. So in the end, Don Giovanni's final damnation is redemptive, a just punishment for all of his sins, transgressions and misdeeds. Mozart's music for the demise of Don Giovanni unhesitatingly treats those forces of supernatural retribution with great solemnity and seriousness. After all, Don Giovanni is in many ways an archetypal hero whose transgressions represent the eternal tragedy of all humanity.

Nevertheless, Mozart added an additional scene to the conclusion of the opera: Act II - Scene 6, or the Epilogue, that serves to lighten the profound seriousness of the final tragedy, and remove the sting from the hero's gruesome descent into Hell. To some, that final scene can be seen as either a gratuitous vaudeville ending to the tragedy, a necessary moralizing sermon, or a moment of cynicism.

Essentially, the six remaining characters announce that with the demise of the evil Don Giovanni, life has returned to normalcy. They remind the audience that Don Giovanni was a classic sinner, the all-time rake who challenged authority, challenged society, and thus challenged God. The survivors tell us that with his demise, justice has been served, and that society has been purged of his seductive and destructive power. But in truth they are all grieving their loss; Don Giovanni may be gone, but he achieved immortality because he will never be forgotten.

For more than two hundred years, Mozart's *Don Giovanni* has caught the imagination of artists, composers, poets, philosophers, psychologists, men of letters, and of course, music lovers.

There is a legacy of inspired literary treatments from Byron, Baudelaire, Mérimée, Pushkin, and Tolstoy. In his Diabelli Variations, the overworked and exploited Beethoven sneered at his publishers by including Leporello's "Notte e giorno faticar" ("I work hard day and night.") In the Prologue to Offenbach's *The Tales of Hoffmann*, there is an underlying suggestion that the whole work is on one level an exegesis of Mozart's opera; after all, Hoffmann, like Don Giovanni, was seeking the ideal love.

Don Octavio's aria, "Il mio tesoro" ("My treasure"), was an early recording sung by John McCormack that supposedly became the most prominent early phonograph recording. Beethoven and Chopin wrote variations on the duet, "Là ci darem la mano"; Liszt included this duet music prominently in his *Don Juan* fantasy; in the film version of *Dorian Grey*, the hero is compelled to hear "Là ci darem la mano" as he embarks on his first seduction; and in James Joyce's *Ulysses*, the music haunts the cuckolded Leopold Bloom after he hears his wife singing it to her lover as they advance toward sexual consummation.

Don Giovanni was a spectacular triumph in Prague; it became, after *Die Entführung aus dem Serail*, the Mozart opera most performed in the composer's lifetime. Since its premiere, nearly every opera singer of note has been associated with one of the main roles in *Don Giovanni.*

Rossini, upon seeing the *Don Giovanni* score for the first time, fell to his knees, kissed the music, and exclaimed of Mozart: "He was God himself." Goethe claimed that only Mozart, the man who had written *Don Giovanni*, was capable of setting his masterpiece *Faust* to music. Gounod, a composer who did set *Faust* to music, said of *Don Giovanni:* "It has been a revelation all my life. For me it is a kind of incarnation of dramatic and musical perfection." Wagner would ask: "Is it possible to find anything more perfect than every piece in *Don Giovanni?* Where else has music individualized and characterized so surely?" Tchaikovsky famously commented, "Through that work I have come to know what music is." Bruno Walter confessed, "I discovered beneath the playfulness a dramatist's inexorable seriousness and wealth of characterization. I recognized in Mozart the Shakespeare of opera." Shaw thought the fine workmanship he found in *Don Giovanni* "the most important part of my education." Kierkegaard exclaimed: "Immortal Mozart, you to whom I owe the fact that I have not gone through life without being profoundly moved."

Don Giovanni provides that great combination of poignant sadness and emotional turmoil, together with moments of lusty charm, comedy, gaiety, excitement, and laughter.

Don Giovanni explains his entire spirit at the beginning of Act II when he defends his life of exploitation and seduction of women to Leporello: "Don't you know that they are more necessary to me than the bread I eat, the very air I breathe."

The underlying essence of the entire opera concerns Don Giovanni's sexual obsessions, a man consumed and resolute in his need to exploit women; for him, it is an indulgence in which the thrill of the chase and the conquest represent the sheer joy and excitement of life itself. Like his fellow libertine, the Duke of Mantua in *Rigoletto*, whose motto was "Questa o quella" ("This woman or that woman)", Don Giovanni's motto was "quest' e quella" ("This woman AND that woman.") Nevertheless, with all of the story's allusions and moral fanfares, in the Mozart/da Ponte opera, Don Giovanni, the owner of the famous catalog, never succeeds in his conquests. In truth, the engine that drove Don Giovanni was his obsession to find the perfect love, but in this story, the great seducer is a recurrent failure.

Listening and seeing Mozart's *Don Giovanni* is a most exciting experience, an opera considered an extraordinary work of genius, a fusion of human, comic and supernatural elements into a great lyric drama.

Mozart was the sovereign master in wedding music to the theater, prompting E.T.A. Hoffmann to call *Don Giovanni* the most perfect opera ever written, "the opera of all operas" — that title unchallenged for more than two centuries.

Don Giovanni

Principal Characters

Brief Story Synopsis

Story Narrative with Music Highlight Examples

Principal Characters in Don Giovanni

Don Giovanni, a licentious Spanish nobleman	Baritone or Bass
Leporello, his servant	Baritone or Bass
Donna Anna, a noble lady	Soprano
The Commendatore (Commandant), Donna Anna's father	Bass
Don Octavio, Donna Anna's fiance	Tenor
Donna Elvira, a noble lady from Burgos, abandoned by Don Giovanni	Soprano
Zerlina, a peasant girl	Soprano
Masetto, Zerlina's fiance	Baritone

TIME: 17th century
PLACE: Seville, Spain

Brief Story Synopsis

The opera story takes place during a 24-hour period, in which Don Giovanni's attempts at seduction encounter interference from avenging victims of his misdeeds: they all seek retribution and punishment for the dissolute rake.

Don Giovanni has surreptitiously entered the apartment of Donna Anna. When he leaves, her screams bring forth her father, the Commandant, who challenges the intruding stranger to a duel. Don Giovanni kills the Commandant, and the grieving daughter, Donna Anna, swears revenge.

Don Giovanni encounters Donna Elvira, a woman he seduced but quickly abandoned; she is determined to convince Don Giovanni to renew their past love. His next attempted conquest is the young country girl, Zerlina, but he is thwarted by the sudden intervention of the avenging Donna Elvira.

Don Giovanni hosts a party for the villagers so that he can have an opportunity to seduce Zerlina, but he is again frustrated by the intervention of the avenging Donna Elvira, Donna Anna, and her fiance Don Octavio.

Leporello, in his master's disguise, courts Donna Elvira so that Don Giovanni can seduce her maid, but a group of vengeful villagers foil his adventure.

Don Giovanni and Leporello escape from their pursuers to a cemetery, where a Statue of the dead Commandant demands that the licentious womanizer repent for his sins. Don Giovanni invites the Statue to dinner. He again refuses the Commandant's demand to repent. Don Giovanni, unable to free himself from the grasp of the Statue, is engulfed by flames and descends into Hell.

Story Narrative with Music Highlight Examples

The Overture to *Don Giovanni* is solemn and foreboding: it is the music that underscores the Commandant's death; the music will reappear in the finale of the opera when the Commandant, now a stone Statue, arrives to dine with Don Giovanni.

Musically, an andante emerges from the key of D minor, and then develops into a brilliant allegro in D major. The Overture music establishes the opera's subtle balance between comedy and tragedy, and also suggests that justice is in pursuit of Don Giovanni, the mercurial seducer.

Act I: Outside Donna Anna's house at night.

Don Giovanni, a noble of Spain, has embarked on another of his daring adventures; he has broken into the house of Don Pedro, the Commandant of Seville, (the Commendatore), in order to seduce his daughter, Donna Anna.

Outside, Don Giovanni's servant, Leporello, stands guard while his master pursues his prey. With rebellious indignation, Leporello complains about his dreadful fate as a servant to his libertine master.

"Notte e giorno faticar"

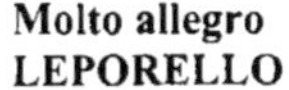

Not - te e gior - no fa - ti - car, per chi nul - la sa gra - dir;
I work hard day and night, and he never thanks me.

Don Giovanni emerges from the palace, pursued by Donna Anna, who is desperately trying to unmask the seducer, and swearing that he will pay dearly for his transgression. After hearing Donna Anna's screams, the Commandant appears to defend his daughter. He raises his sword and challenges the anonymous intruder. In reluctant self-defense, Don Giovanni duels with the Commandant and mortally wounds him. Seemingly unmoved by the corpse on the ground, Don Giovanni escapes from the palace with Leporello.

Donna Anna discovers her dead father and becomes horrified. She unites with her fiance, Don Octavio, to vow revenge against the murderer; they express their relentless determination to pursue the unknown criminal and bring him to justice.

"Fuggi crudele"

Fug - gi, crudele, fuggi! la - scia,che mora an - ch'io
Leave me, cruel man, leave me! Let me die too!

A street in Seville. It is early morning.

Don Giovanni and Leporello roam the city in search of new conquests. They notice a beautiful woman: it is Donna Elvira. She is heard expressing her sadness and outrage at Don Giovanni's treachery. She is hopeful that her faithless lover will return to her, but vows that if she fails, she will inflict torture on him.

"Ah! chi mi dice mai quel barbaro dov'é?"

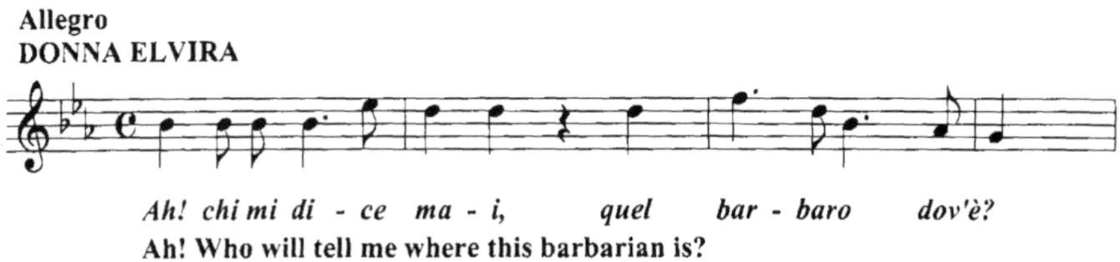

Don Giovanni, unaware of Donna Elvira's identity, approaches the lady in distress. But before he can offer her consolation, he finds to his consternation that she is none other than Donna Elvira of Burgos, the woman he had spurned recently; likewise, Donna Elvira recognizes the perfidious Don Giovanni.

Don Giovanni tries to persuade Donna Elvira that he had justifiable reasons for abandoning her, but Donna Elvira refuses to believe her betrayer or accept his explanations. Don Giovanni quietly escapes from the impassioned Donna Elvira, leaving Leporello to console her anguish.

Leporello pleads with the spurned woman to dispel her anger: she is far from the first or the last woman to be jilted by his profligate master. With cynical pride, Leporello reads Donna Elvira his master's bulky catalogue of conquests and seductions: in Italy 640, Germany 231, France 100, Turkey 91, but in Spain 1003.

"Madamina! Il catalogo è questo"

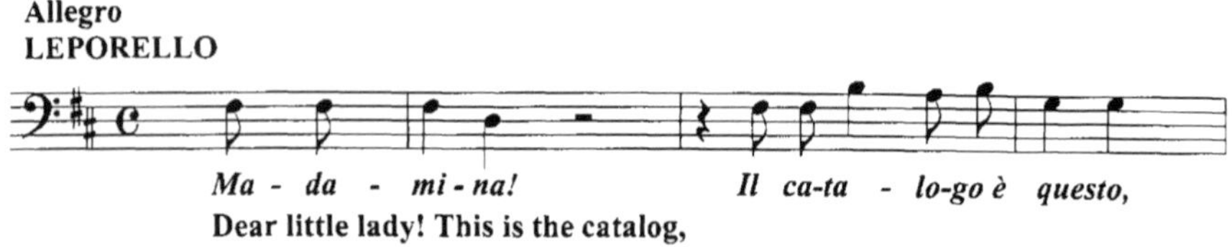

Leporello tries to persuade Donna Elvira that his master is unworthy of her passion, but he is unsuccessful.

He runs off, leaving the spurned and disheartened Donna Elvira alone in her sorrow and grief.

In the countryside near Don Giovanni's palace.

Country folk sing, dance, and praise the joys of life and love. Don Giovanni mingles with the peasants and becomes enamored by Zerlina, a beautiful young woman engaged to marry Masetto. Don Giovanni envisions Zerlina as his next conquest; he generously offers to place her forthcoming marriage under his "protection."

Don Giovanni invites all the peasants to his palace, instructing Leporello to find diversion for the bridegroom, Masetto, so he can be free to court Zerlina. Discretion becomes the better part of valor as Leporello escorts the protesting Masetto into the palace. But Masetto explodes in frustration and outrage because he must accede to authority: " Ho capito, Signor, sì" ("Yes, my lord, I understand you.")

Alone with Zerlina, Don Giovanni tries to seduce her with a serenade. He suggests that they escape to a little house on the estate where they can be alone; he promises to marry Zerlina.

"Là ci darem la mano, là mi dirai di sì"

Just as Zerlina is about to surrender to Don Giovanni's seductive charms, Donna Elvira suddenly appears, the jealous and spurned woman congratulating herself on arriving at such an opportune time to save an innocent girl. Donna Elvira proceeds to launch a tirade of denunciations against the profligate Don Giovanni.

Zerlina listens anxiously, and then questions Don Giovanni if Donna Elvira's accusations are true. With feigned compassion, Don Giovanni explains that the poor and unfortunate Donna Elvira is in love with him, and because of his kindness and selflessness, he has had to placate her by pretending to love her.

With fury and indignation, Donna Elvira warns Zerlina to beware that this man will betray her with lies and worthless promises. Donna Elvira seizes Zerlina and leads her away under her protection, further warning her that she must defend her honor against this lecherous nobleman.

" Ah! fuggi il traditor!"

Don Octavio and Donna Anna appear. Donna Anna does not recognize her assailant from the night before, and unwittingly solicits Don Giovanni's help and friendship in her quest for revenge.

Donna Elvira suddenly appears, crying out dramatically: "So, I find you again, perfidious monster!" Donna Elvira proceeds to warn Donna Anna not to have faith in this man who would betray her: "Non ti fidar, o misera" ("Do not have faith in this miserable man.")

Donna Anna and Don Octavio become moved by Donna Elvira's tears: aside, Don Giovanni tells them that the poor woman is mad, but perhaps he can calm her. Donna Anna and Don Octavio become confused and do not know whom to believe. As Donna Elvira storms away, Don Giovanni announces that he must follow the poor unfortunate woman, his excuse to bid farewell to Donna Anna and Don Octavio.

Donna Anna has a revelation; upon hearing Don Giovanni's voice, she is now convinced that he was her assailant and the murderer of her father. As an attentive and curious Don Octavio listens, Donna Anna proceeds to narrate the details of the previous evening, all the while imploring Don Octavio to join her in revenge.

"Or sai, chi l'onore rapire a me volse"

Andante
DONNA ANNA

After Donna Anna's furious proclamations of revenge, she storms away, leaving Don Octavio alone to reflect on her agony. He is confounded by the events, unable to believe that such a nobleman could be capable of so black a crime.

But as Donna's lover and friend, he swears that it his duty to vindicate Donna Anna's honor.

"Dalla sua pace"

DON OTTAVIO

A terrace before Don Giovanni's palace.

Don Giovanni, obsessed in his pursuit of Zerlina, has invited all the peasants to his palace for a night of merriment.

Don Giovanni commands Leporello to round up the guests and prepare food, wine and entertainment for all.

"Finch'han dal vino calda"

Meanwhile, Zerlina argues with her jealous fiance Masetto, who has accused her of being unfaithful and abandoning him on their wedding day.

Zerlina proclaims her innocence, and tries to pacify her outraged fiance, even inviting him to beat her for her presumed insolence.

"Batti, batti, o bel Masetto"

Don Giovanni arrives in an expansive and hospitable mood. He finds Zerlina and persuades her to disappear with him into the arbor, but his intrigue is thwarted when he finds the implacable Masetto hiding there. In frustration, Don Giovanni escorts them both to the festivities in the palace.

The ballroom in Don Giovanni's palace.

Suddenly, a trio of masked intruders arrive: they are the avenging Donna Anna, Don Octavio, and Donna Elvira, all determined to invade the ball, capture Don Giovanni, expose his wickedness, and punish him.

Leporello advises Don Giovanni that the three masquerading characters seem to be guests. Don Giovanni instructs Leporello to welcomes them to the ball.

The Minuet:

The three masked avengers join the dancing at the ball. Don Giovanni pursues the apprehensive Zerlina; after he coerces her, both disappear through one of the ballroom doors into another room.

Suddenly, Zerlina is heard screaming. The dancing stops and the three masked avengers take the initiative to break down the door to rescue Zerlina. After Zerlina is returned to safety the avengers advance upon Don Giovanni, crying out: "Tremble! Soon the whole world will know of your black and terrible deed, and of your inhuman cruelty. Hark to the thunder of vengeance!"

Don Giovanni grabs the incredulous Leporello and accuses him of being the seducer. Then Don Giovanni announces that he fears nothing and nobody; with Leporelloo at his side, he forces his way past the avengers, and both escape.

Act II: In front of Donna Elvira's house.

In a moment of pleading righteousness, Leporello threatens to leave Don Giovanni's service, urging his master to give up his profligate life-style. But Don Giovanni defends himself philosophically, claiming that seduction is the bread of his life. He gives money to Leporello, temporarily assuaging the rebellious servant.

Don Giovanni has now become fascinated with Donna Elvira's maid. But to succeed in this new adventure, he must draw Donna Elvira away: Don Giovanni and Leporello exchange cloaks and hats, and Leporello, now disguised as his master, is commanded to court Donna Elvira.

Donna Elvira appears at her window, and reflects on her confused feelings: she prays that her heart would stop yearning for the man she knows is a deceiver, but the man she cannot stop loving.

Don Giovanni stands in the shadows behind Leporello, who is now dressed in his master's cloak and hat. Don Giovanni, the voice behind Leporello, responds to the vulnerable Donna Elvira with seductive flattery and endearments; he begs for forgiveness and promises her faithful love. Donna Elvira's resistance and defenses immediately break down. She rushes from her balcony to join the man she believes is Don Giovanni, who has returned to reciprocate her love.

Donna Elvira emerges from the house and passionately embraces her lover (Leporello), the servant clearly enjoying the charade and the impersonation of his master. Don Giovanni creates a disturbance, a cue for Leporello to flee the scene with the frightened Donna Elvira. With Donna Elvira gone, Don Giovanni is left alone to serenade Elvira's maid.

"Deh vieni alla finestra, o mio tesoro"

Don Giovanni's attempted romantic escapade with Donna Elvira's maid is interrupted by a band of armed peasants who are searching for him: their leader is the pistol-waving Masetto. But Don Giovanni is not recognized because he is still in the disguise of his servant, Leporello. The peasants take him into their confidence. Don Giovanni proceeds to give them false directions to find the rascal: the peasants leave, scattering throughout the city in search of Don Giovanni.

But at Don Giovanni's insistence, Masetto remains behind. Don Giovanni invites the naive young man to show him his weapons. When Masetto hands over his musket and pistol, he is defenseless. Don Giovanni thrashes him violently before disappearing into the night.

Zerlina arrives to discover Masetto groaning in pain. She gives him solace, and promises him a cure that will restore him to health: the cure is her love.

"Vedrai, carino, se sei bonino"

A dark courtyard before Donna Anna's house.

Leporello leads the apprehensive Donna Elvira into a darkened courtyard to seek refuge from their pursuers. Donna Anna, Don Octavio, and then Zerlina and Masetto appear, all of them still in search of Don Giovanni. But they believe that they have discovered him (Leporello in disguise) and demand death to the perfidious villain. The unfortunate servant is terrified and pleads for his life. Zerlina binds him to a chair, but miraculously, he escapes.

Alone, Don Octavio vows to comfort his beloved by bringing Don Giovanni to justice.

"Il mio tesoro"

Andante grazioso
DON OCTAVIO

Il mio te - so - ro in - tan - to,
Meanwhile, my dearest treasure, console yourself,

Donna Elvira, in a moment of self-pity, again expresses her sadness and anguish at Don Giovanni's betrayal of her.

"Mi tradi quell'anima ingrata"

Allegro assai
DONNA ELVIRA

Mi tra - dì quell' al - ma in gra - ta, quell' al - ma in - gra - ta,
Oh God, that ungrateful soul betrayed me.

A cemetery with equestrian statues, among them the marble statue of the Commandant.

Don Giovanni and Leporello, fugitives from all the pursuing avengers, meet in the safety of a cemetery. Suddenly, they are interrupted by a sinister voice coming from a stone Statue: "Your jests will turn to woe before morning!"

Looking around, Don Giovanni notices the Commandant's statue and commands Leporello to read its inscription: "Vengeance here awaits the villain who took my life." Don Giovanni instructs Leporello to invite the Statue to supper. The Statue nods its head in acceptance, and then Don Giovanni personally extends his invitation: the Statue accepts with a solemn "yes."

Don Giovanni, burning with defiance, goes home to prepare for the arrival of his strange guest. Leporello accompanies him, terrified and sensing doom.

A room in Donna Anna's house.

Donna Anna continues to grieve for her father, advising the consoling Don Octavio that they cannot wed until her father's murder has been avenged. Don Octavio interprets her postponement as cruelty, but Donna Anna defends her need to grieve for her loss.

"Non mi dir, bell' idol mio"

Larghetto
DONNA ANNA

Non mi dir, bell' - i - dol mi - o,
Don't tell me, my dear, that I am cruel to you.

In an expansive and hospitable mood, Don Giovanni dines in his palace while being entertained by musicians.

Donna Elvira, agitated and desperate, again appears; she promises to forgive Don Giovanni if he would change his profligate life-style. She falls to her knees before Don Giovanni and pleads with him to repent, but Don Giovanni loses his patience and dismisses her: as the spurned Donna Elvira leaves, she curses Don Giovanni as a "horrible example of iniquity."

When a knocking is heard at the door, a fearful Leporello hides under a table. Don Giovanni opens the door; before him is the Statue of the Commandant.

The Statue refuses Don Giovanni's offer to dine with him. He grasps Don Giovanni's hand and urges him to mend his ways and repent. Don Giovanni struggles frantically and in vain to free himself from the Statue's grip; he remains defiant and refuses to repent.

Flames envelop the hall as the voices of demons are heard condemning and denouncing Don Giovanni. With a final cry of despair, Don Giovanni is swallowed up by the engulfing fires of Hell.

Epilogue:

The avengers have seemingly been victorious. Masetto and Zerlina, Don Octavio and Donna Anna, and the lonely Donna Elvira, are unanimous in their lustful eagerness to show their contempt and hatred for the perfidious Don Giovanni.

Leporello provides them with a detailed account of the horrible events which caused the demise of his master.

Donna Anna and Don Octavio suggest that all their troubles have been resolved by divine intervention. She advises Don Octavio that she will remain in mourning for an entire year, her marriage to him therefore postponed and to be reconsidered afterwards.

Donna Elvira announces that she will retire to a convent.

Zerlina and Masetto decide to return home to dine together.

Leporello declares that he has but one practical alternative: he will go to the tavern and seek a new master.

All celebrate the demise of the sinner: divine justice has been triumphed!

Don Giovanni

Libretto

ACT I - Scene 1

A square in Seville. It is night. In front of the palace of the Commandant, Leporello, holding a lantern, moves about cautiously and impatiently.

Molto allegro
LEPORELLO

Not - te e gior - no fa - ti - car, per chi nul - la sa gra - dir;

Leporello:
Notte e giorno faticar,
per chi nulla sa gradir,
piova e vento sopportar,
mangiar male e mal dormir.

Leporello:
I work hard day and night,
and he never thanks me.
I endure winds and rain,
poor food and little sleep.

Voglio far il gentiluomo!
E non voglio più servir.
Oh che caro galantuomo!

I want to be a gentleman!
And I no longer want to be a servant.
Oh what a gallant man!

Vuol star dentro colla bella,
ed io far la sentinella!
Voglio far il gentiluomo
e non voglio più servir.

He's inside with his conquest,
and I am the sentry!
I want to be a gentleman
and I no longer want to be a servant.

Ma mi par che venga gente;
non mi voglio far sentir.

But it seems that someone is coming;
I don't want to be seen here.

As Leporello hides, Don Giovanni enters, followed by Donna Anna, who holds his arm firmly.

Donna Anna:
Non sperar, se non m'uccidi,
ch'io ti lasci fuggir mai!

Donna Anna:
Don't hope, even if you kill me,
I won't let you escape!

Don Giovanni:
Donna folle! In darno gridi,
chi son io tu non saprai!

Don Giovanni: *(concealing his features)*
Foolish woman! Vain cries!
You'll never know who I am!

Leporello:
Che tumulto! Oh ciel, che gridi!
Il padron in nuovi guai.

Leporello:
What shouting! Heavens, what screaming!
My master's in some new trouble!

Donna Anna:
Gente! Servi! Al traditore!

Donna Anna:
People! Servants! A traitor!

Don Giovanni:
(Taci e trema al mio furore!)

Don Giovanni: *(covering her mouth)*
(Be silent, or you'll experience my anger!)

Donna Anna:
Scellerato!

Donna Anna:
Villain!

Don Giovanni:
Sconsigliata!

Don Giovanni:
Imprudent woman!

Leporello:
Sta a veder che il malandrino mi farà precipitar!

Leporello:
Look how this libertine will bring about my downfall!

Donna Anna:
Come furia disperata ti saprò perseguitar!

Donna Anna:
I'm desperate to know who this pursuer is!

Don Giovanni:
(Questa furia disperata mi vuol far precipitar!)

Don Giovanni:
(She'll make me do something frightful!)

Donna Anna's father, the Commandant, approaches. Donna Anna rushes into the palace. The Commandant holds a torch in one hand, and a sword in the other.

Il Commendatore:
Lasciala, indegno! Battiti meco!

Commandant:
Leave her alone! Fight me!

Don Giovanni:
Va, non mi degno di pugnar teco.

Don Giovanni:
Go, I don't want to fight you.

Il Commendatore:
Così pretendi da me fuggir?

Commandant:
Do you think you can get away like a coward?

Leporello:
(Potessi almeno di qua partir!)

Leporello:
(I wish I could get away from here!)

Don Giovanni:
Misero, attendi, se vuoi morir!

Don Giovanni: *(draws his sword)*
Wretch, stand there if you want to die!

The Commandant attacks Don Giovanni.
After Don Giovanni strikes the Commandant with his sword, he falls, mortally wounded.

Il Commendatore:
Ah, soccorso! Son tradito!
L'assassino m'ha ferito,
e dal seno palpitante,
sento l'anima partir.

Commandant:
Ah help! I've been betrayed!
The assassin has wounded me,
and I feel that I am dying.
I feel my soul leaving me.

The Commandant dies. Servants rush from the palace.

Don Giovanni:
Ah, già cade il sciagurato,
affannoso e agonizzante,
già dal seno palpitante
veggo l'anima partir.

Don Giovanni:
The meddling fool lies prostrate,
agonizing and without breath.
His breast throbs,
and I see his soul parting.

Leporello:
Qual misfatto! Qual eccesso!
Entro il sen dallo spavento
palpitar il cor mi sento!
Io non so che far, che dir.

Leporello:
What a horror! What debauchery!
The ghost enters my breast
and I feel my heart throbbing!
I don't know what to do or say.

Don Giovanni and Leporello leave hastily.

Don Giovanni:
Leporello, ove sei?

Don Giovanni: *(in a low voice)*
Leporello, where are you?

Leporello:
Son qui, per mia disgrazia, e voi?

Leporello:
Here, unfortunately. And you?

Don Giovanni:
Son qui.

Don Giovanni:
I'm here.

Leporello:
Chi è morto, voi o il vecchio?

Leporello:
Who's dead, you or the old man?

Don Giovanni:
Che domanda da bestia! Il vecchio.

Don Giovanni:
What a foolish question! The old man.

Leporello:
Bravo, due imprese leggiadre!
Sforzar la figlia ed ammazzar il padre!

Leporello:
Great, two impressive exploits!
Seduce the daughter, and murder the father!

Don Giovanni:
L'ha voluto, suo danno.

Don Giovanni:
He willed his ruin.

Leporello:
Ma Donn'Anna, cosa ha voluto?

Leporello:
And did Donna Anna will her's too?

Don Giovanni:
Taci, non mi seccar, vien meco, se non vuoi
qualche cosa ancor tu!

Don Giovanni: *(threatening Leporello)*
Quiet, don't question me.
Come with me unless you want the same fate!

Leporello:
Non vo'nulla, Signor, non parlo più.

Leporello:
I want nothing. Sir, I'll say no more.

Both Don Giovanni and Leporello depart.

In agitation, Donna Anna and Don Octavio descend the palace steps. They are followed by servants bearing torches.

Donna Anna:
Ah, del padre in periglio in soccorso voliam.

Donna Anna:
Ah, my father is in danger, let's hurry to help him.

Don Ottavio:
Tutto il mio sangue verserò, se bisogna.
Ma dov'è il scellerato?

Don Octavio: *(raising his sword)*
I'll shed my last drop of my blood, if necessary. But where is the scoundrel?

Donna Anna:
In questo loco. Ma qual mai s'offre.

Donna Anna:
Here in the palace.

Donna Anna sees her father, and throws herself on the corpse.

O Dei, spettacolo funesto agli occhi miei!
Il padre! Padre mio! Mio caro padre!

But heavens, what a horrible sight before me! Father! My dear father!

Don Ottavio:
Signore!

Don Octavio:
My lord!

Donna Anna:
Ah, l'assassino mel trucidò.
Quel sangue, quella piaga, quel volto,
tinto, e coperto del color di morte,
ei non respira più fredde ha le membra
padre mio!
Caro padre! Padre amato! Io manco, io moro.

Donna Anna:
Ah, the assassin murdered him.
That blood, the wound, his face covered and stained. He has the pallor of death.
My father! He no longer breathes, and his limbs are cold! Dear father!
Beloved father! I am fainting. I am dying.

Donna Anna faints momentarily, and then Don Octavio raises her and seats her.

Don Ottavio:
Ah, soccorrete, amici, il mio tesoro!
Cercatemi, recatemi qualche odor, qualche spirito.
Ah! Non tardate. Donn'Anna! Sposa!
Amica! Il duolo estremo la meschinella uccide.

Don Octavio: *(calling servants)*
My friends, help me with my beloved!
Fetch water, some scents, some spirits.

Please hurry. Donna Anna! My beloved!
Her intense grief is destroying her.

Donna Anna:
Ahi!

Donna Anna: *(after being restored by smelling salts) Ah,* me!

Don Ottavio:
Già rinviene. Datele nuovi aiuti.

Don Octavio:
She's reviving. Give her more help.

Donna Anna:
Padre mio!

Donna Anna: *(sighing despairingly)*
My father!

Don Ottavio:
Celate, allontanate agli occhi suoi quell'oggetto d'orrore. Anima mia, consolati, fa core.

Don Octavio: *(to the servants)*
Quickly remove her from this scene of horror. Dear love, console yourself and be strong.

Servants remove the Commandant's body into the palace.

Donna Anna:
Fuggi, crudele, fuggi!
Lascia che mora anch'io
ora che è morto, oh Dio!
Chi a me la vita diè!

Donna Anna: *(repulsing Don Octavio)*
Leave me, cruel man, leave me!
Let me die too!
Oh God, the man who brought me life
is now dead!

Don Ottavio:
Senti, cor mio, deh! Senti;
guardami un solo istante!
Ti parla il caro amante,
che vive sol per te.

Don Octavio:
Listen, my beloved, listen!
Look at me for just one moment!
Your dear lover speaks to you,
the man who lives only for you.

Donna Anna:
Tu sei! Perdon, mio bene.
L'affanno mio, le pene.
Ah! Il padre mio dov'è?

Donna Anna: *(apologetically)*
You are indeed my love! Forgive me!
I have such anguish and pain.
Ah! Father where are you?

Don Ottavio:
Il padre?
Lascia, o cara, la rimembranza amara.
Hai sposo e padre in me.

Don Octavio:
Your father?
Abandon that bitter thought.
You have both husband and father in me.

Donna Anna:
Ah! Vendicar, se il puoi,
giura quel sangue ognor!

Donna Anna:
If you can avenge me,
swear it on this honorable blood!

Don Ottavio:
Lo giuro agli occhi tuoi, lo giuro al nostro amor!

Don Octavio: *(raising his hand as if taking an oath)* I swear it before your eyes.
I swear it by our love!

A due:
Che giuramento, o dei!
Che barbaro momento!
Tra cento affetti e cento vammi
ondeggiando il cor.

Both:
That us our vow, oh Gods!
What a horrible moment!
So much emotion and grief
stir in my heart.

Both enter the palace.

ACT I - Scene 2

A street in Seville. It is early morning.

Don Giovanni:
Orsù, spicciati presto. Cosa vuoi?

Don Giovanni:
Hurry up. What do you want?

Leporello:
L'affar di cui si tratta è importante.

Leporello:
What I am about to speak about is important.

Don Giovanni:
Lo credo.

Don Giovanni:
No doubt.

Leporello:
È importantissimo.

Leporello:
It's very important.

Don Giovanni:
Meglio ancora. Finiscila.

Don Giovanni:
Better yet. Get to the point.

Leporello:
Giurate di non andar in collera.

Leporello:
Swear not to get angry.

Don Giovanni:
Lo giuro sul mio onore, purché non parli del Commendatore.

Don Giovanni:
I swear it on my honor, as long as you don't mention the Commandant.

Leporello:
Siamo soli?

Leporello:
Are we alone?

Don Giovanni:
Lo vedo.

Don Giovanni:
I believe so.

Leporello:
Nessun ci sente?

Leporello:
No one can hear us?

Don Giovanni:
Via!

Don Giovanni:
Go ahead!

Leporello:
Vi posso dire tutto liberamente?

Leporello:
Can I speak freely?

Don Giovanni:
Sì.

Don Giovanni:
You may.

Leporello:
Dunque quando è così, caro signor padrone, la vita che menate è da briccone!

Leporello:
Well, if that's the case, my dear master, the life you are leading is disgraceful!

Don Giovanni:
Temerario, in tal guisa!

Don Giovanni:
How dare you talk to me that way!

Leporello:
E il giuramento!

Leporello:
But you promised!

Don Giovanni:
Non so di giuramenti. Taci, o ch'io...

Don Giovanni: *(threateningly)*
I know of no promises. Quiet, or I....

Leporello:
Non parlo più, non fiato, o padron mio!

Leporello:
Master, I'll say no more, not another breath!

Don Giovanni:
Così saremo amici. Ora dì un poco: sai tu perché son qui?

Don Giovanni:
So now we can be friends. Listen, do you know why I'm here?

Leporello:
Non ne so nulla.
Ma essendo l'alba chiara, non sarebbe qualche nuova conquista?
Io lo devo saper per porla in lista.

Leporello:
I've no idea.
But it's a clear morning. Do you have some new conquest? You must tell me the lady's name so I can put her in my list.

Don Giovanni:
Va là, che sei il grand'uom!
Sappi ch'io sono innamorato d'una bella dama, e son certo che m'ama.
La vidi, le parlai; meco al casino questa notte verrà.
Zitto, mi pare sentire odor di femmina!

Don Giovanni:
Spoken like an intelligent man!
You must know that I'm in love with a most beautiful woman, and I'm sure she loves me. I've seen her and talked to her.
She's to meet me at the country house.
Quiet, I seem to smell the aroma of a woman!

Leporello:
(Cospetto, che odorato perfetto!)

Leporello:
(Wow, what a perfect sense of smell!)

Don Giovanni:
All'aria mi par bella.

Don Giovanni:
Her fragrance seems to be beautiful.

Leporello:
(E che occhio, dico!)

Leporello:
(And what an eye he has!)

Don Giovanni:
Ritiriamoci un poco, e scopriamo terren.

Don Giovanni:
Let's hide ourselves for a while, and check things out.

Leporello:
(Già prese foco!)

Leporello:
(He's already on fire!)

As Don Giovanni and Leporello conceal themselves, Donna Elvira approaches.

Donna Elvira:
Ah, chi mi dice mai
quel barbaro dov'è,
che per mio scorno amai,
che mi mancò di fe?

Ah, se ritrovo l'empio
e a me non torna ancor,
vo' farne orrendo scempio,
gli vo' cavare il cor.

Donna Elvira:
Ah, who will tell me
where that traitor is?
How could I love such a man
who betrayed my faith?

But if I find the traitor,
and if he doesn't return to me,
I'll inflict havoc on him,
and tear his heart out.

Don Giovanni:
Udisti? Qualche bella dal vago abbandonata.
Poverina! Cerchiam di consolare il suo tormento.

Don Giovanni: *(softly to Leporello)*
Do you hear? This fair damsel is complaining of some faithless lover.
Poor girl! I must try to console her anguish.

Leporello:
(Così ne consolò mile e ottocento).

Leporello:
(Like the way he consoled one thousand eight hundred!)

Don Giovanni:
Signorina! Signorina!

Don Giovanni: *(boldly approaching Donna Elvira) Miss*! Miss!

Donna Elvira:
Chi è là?

Donna Elvira:
Who is there?

Don Giovanni:
Stelle! Che vedo!

Don Giovanni:
Good Heavens! Who do I see?

Leporello:
(O bella! Donna Elvira!)

Leporello:
(Oh, it's the beautiful Donna Elvira!)

Donna Elvira:
Don Giovanni! Sei qui?
Mostro! Fellon! Nido d'inganni!

Donna Elvira:
Don Giovanni! You here!
Monster! Criminal! Deceiver!

Leporello:
(Che titoli cruscanti!
Manco male che lo conosce bene!)

Leporello:
(What choice epithets!
She certainly knows him well!)

Don Giovanni:
Via, cara Donna Elvira, calmate quella collera! Sentite, lasciatemi parlar!

Don Giovanni:
Come, dear Elvira, calm your fury!
Listen, let me speak!

Donna Elvira:
Cosa puoi dire, dopo azion sì nera?
In casa mia entri furtivamente.
A forza d'arte, di giuramenti e di lusinghe arrivi a sedurre il cor mio; m'innamori, o crudele!

Mi dichiari tua sposa, e poi, mancando della terra e del ciel al santo dritto,
con enorme delitto dopo tre dì da Burgos t'allontani.
M'abbandoni, mi fuggi, e lasci in preda al rimorso ed al pianto, per pena forse che t'amai cotanto!

Donna Elvira:
What can you say after such awful behavior? You entered my house secretly. You used cunning, flattery, and promises to seduce my heart; I fell in love with you, you cruel man!

You declared me your wife, and then, you defied the holy laws of heaven and earth and denied my sacred right; after three days you abandoned me in Burgos. You abandoned me, you fled, and left me in remorse and tears, my punishment because I loved you so much!

Leporello:
(Pare un libro stampato!)

Leporello:
(She echoes the printed romances!)

Don Giovanni:
Oh, in quanto a questo, ebbi le mie ragioni!
È vero?

Don Giovanni:
As to those concerns, I had my reasons for doing it! Didn't I, Leporello?

Leporello:
È vero! E che ragioni forti!

Leporello: *(ironically)*
You certainly did! Very important reasons!

Donna Elvira:
E quali sono, se non la tua perfidia, la leggerezza tua? Ma il giusto cielo volle ch'io ti trovassi, per far le sue, le mie vendette.

Donna Elvira:
What can they be other than your perfidy and reckless inconsideration? But the righteous heavens wanted me to find you, to impose their revenge and mine.

Don Giovanni:
Eh via! Siate più ragionevole!
(Mi pone a cimento costei!)
Se non credete a labbro mio, credete a questo galantuomo.

Don Giovanni:
Come now! Be more reasonable!
(This woman embarrasses me!)
If you don't believe me, believe this trustworthy gentleman.

Leporello:
(Salvo il vero.)

Leporello:
(I'll vow the truth.)

Don Giovanni:
Via, dille un poco.

Don Giovanni:
Come here and tell her something.

Leporello:
E cosa devo dirle?

Leporello: *(aside to Giovanni)*
And what am I to tell her?

Don Giovanni:
Sì, sì, dille pur tutto.

Don Giovanni:
Yes, yes, explain everything.

Donna Elvira does not notice that Don Giovanni has fled.

Donna Elvira:
Ebben, fa presto!

Donna Elvira: *(to Leporello)*
Well, tell me right away!

Leporello:
Madama, veramente, in questo mondo conciò, sia cosa, quando, fosse che, il quadro non è tondo.

Leporello: *(hesitating)*
Madam, truthfully, most assuredly in the strange world in which we live, it may be safely asserted that a square is not a circle.

Donna Elvira:
Sciagurato! Così del mio dolor giuoco? Ti prendi? Ah voi!

Donna Elvira:
You scoundrel! Are you mocking my grief? And you, Don Giovanni.

Donna Elvira suddenly discovers that Don Giovanni has gone.

Stelle! L'iniquo fuggì! Misera me! Dov'è? In qual parte?

Heavens! The wicked one fled! Poor me! Where is he? Which way did he go?

Leporello:
Eh! Lasciate che vada. Egli non merita che di lui ci pensiate.

Leporello:
Ah, let him go! He doesn't deserve your thoughts.

Donna Elvira:
Il scellerato m'ingannò, mi tradì.

Donna Elvira:
The scoundrel deceived and betrayed me!

Leporello:
Eh! Consolatevi; non siete voi,
non foste, e non sa retenè la prima,
né l'ultima.

Leporello:
Console yourself! You are not the first
woman he has deserted,
And neither will you be the last.

Guardate: questo non picciol libro è tutto pieno dei nomi di sue belle.
Ogni villa, ogni borgo, ogni paese è testimon di sue donnesche imprese.

Look! This large book is filled entirely with the names of his conquests.
Every village, every town, and every country has witnessed his impressive exploits.

Leporello takes a large list from his pocket:
the catalog of Don Giovanni's exploits.

Allegro
LEPORELLO

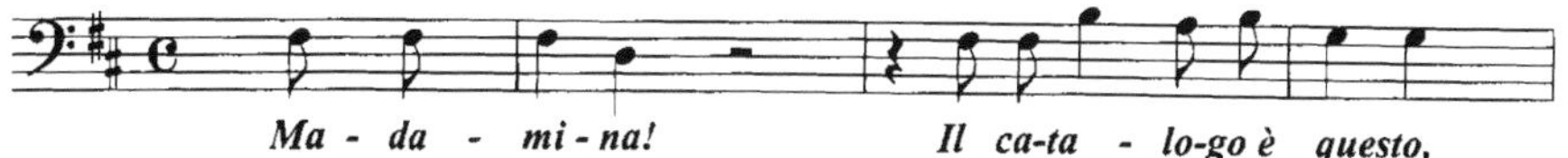

Madamina! Il catalogo è questo
delle belle che amò il padron mio;
un catalogo egli è che ho fatt'io;
osservate, leggete con me!
In Italia seicento e quaranta;
in Almagna duecento e trent'una;
cento in Francia, in Turchia novantina;
ma in Ispagna son già mille e tre!

Dear little lady! This is the catalog
of the beautiful women my master has
loved; a catalog I made myself.
Look at it, and read it with me!
In Italy 640;
in Germany 231;
100 in France, and in Turkey 91;
but in Spain, there are already 1003!

V'han fra queste contadine,
cameriere, cittadine.
V'han contesse, baronesse,
Marchesine, principesse.
E v'han donne d'ogni grado,
d'ogni forma, d'ogni età!

Among these, there are peasant girls,
waitresses, and town girls.
There are Countesses and Baronesses,
Marchionesses and Princesses.
There have been women of every rank,
every shape, and every age!

Nella bionda egli ha l'usanza
di lodar la gentilezza.
Nella bruna la costanza,
nella bianca la dolcezza.

With the blond women, it's his custom
to praise their gentleness.
With the dark haired, their fidelity,
and with the gray haired, their sweetness.

Vuol d'inverno la grassotta,
vuol d'estate la magrotta.
È la grande maestosa,
la piccina e ognor vezzosa.

In winter he wants them plump,
But in summer he wants them lean.
He is always charming to the big ladies
as well as the small.

Delle vecchie fa conquista
pel piacer di porle in lista.
Sua passion predominante
è la giovin principiante.

He conquers the old ones
for the pleasure of adding them to the list.
But his predominant passion
is the young beginner.

Non si pica, se sia ricca,
se sia brutta, se sia bella.
Purché porti la gonnella,
voi sapete quel che fa.

He doesn't mind if she's rich,
or ugly, or beautiful.
You know what he does,
providing she wears a skirt.

Leporello leaves hastily.

Donna Elvira:
In questa forma dunque mi tradì il scellerato!

Donna Elvira:
This is the way that scoundrel betrayed me!

È questo il premio che quel barbaro rende all'amor mio?
Ah! Vendicar vogl'io l'ingannato mio cor!
Pria ch'ei mi fugga si ricorra, si vada,
io sento in petto sol vendetta parlar, rabbia e dispetto!

Is this the way that barbarian returns my affection?
Ah! I want revenge for my deceived heart!
Before he escapes me, I'll have recourse.
I feel only revenge in my heart, rage and malice!

Elvira departs.

ACT I - Scene 3

The open country with a view of Don Giovanni's palace.
Zerlina, Masetto, and a group of peasants sing and dance.

Zerlina:
Giovinette che fate all'amore,
non lasciate che passi l'età!
Se nel seno vi bulica il core,
il rimedio vedetelo qua!
Fa la la, la la la, la la la!
Che piacer, che piacer che sarà!

Zerlina:
Pretty lasses, indulge in love,
and don't let your youth fly by!
If the flames burn in your heart,
the remedy is here!
Fa la la, la la la, la la la!
What pleasure, what pleasure there will be!

Coro:
Ah, che piacer, che piacer che sarà!
Fa la la...

Chorus:
What pleasure, what pleasure there will be!
Fa la la....

Masetto:
Giovinetti leggeri di testa,
non andate girando di là.
Poco dura de'matti la festa,
ma per me cominciato non ha.
Fa la la, la la la, la la la!
Che piacer, che piacer che sarà!

Masetto:
Boys, don't keep spinning around because your heads will not be clear.
The mad party will last a while,
but for me, it hasn't begun.
Fa la la, la, la la, la la la!
What pleasures, what pleasure there will be!

Zerlina e Masetto:
Vieni, vieni, carino, godiamo,
e cantiamo e balliamo e suoniamo!
Che piacer, che piacer che sarà!

Zerlina and Masetto:
Come, come, dearest, let's enjoy ourselves,
and let's sing, dance, and dream!
What pleasure, what pleasure there will be!

Coro:
Fa la la, la la la, la la la!
Che piacer, che piacer che sarà!

Chorus:
Fa la la, la la la, fa la la!
What pleasure, what pleasure there will be!

Don Giovanni and Leporello arrive.

Don Giovanni: (Manco male, è partita.) Oh guarda, che bella gioventù; che belle donne!	**Don Giovanni:** (Thank God, she is gone.) Look, what beautiful young and pretty girls!
Leporello: (Fra tante, per mia fè, vi sarà qualche cosa anche per me.)	**Leporello:** (I have faith that soon one of them might be for me.)
Don Giovanni: Cari amici, buon giorno! Seguitate a stare allegramente, seguite a suonar, buona gente! C'è qualche sposalizio?	**Don Giovanni:** *(interrupting Zerlina and Masetto)* Dear friends, good morning! Good people, continue to enjoy yourselves and continue to play! Is there going to be a wedding?
Zerlina: Sì, signore, e la sposa son io.	**Zerlina:** *(bowing politely to Don Giovanni)* Yes, sir, and I am the bride.
Don Giovanni: Me ne consolo. Lo sposo?	**Don Giovanni:** I'm happy for you. Where is the bridegroom?
Masetto: Io, per servirla.	**Masetto:** Here, at your service.
Don Giovanni: Oh bravo! Per servirmi; questo è vero parlar da galantuomo.	**Don Giovanni:** How wonderful! Spoken like a gallant man who serves me.
Leporello: (Basta che sia marito!)	**Leporello:** (As long as he remains the husband and not the cuckold!)
Zerlina: Oh, il mio Masetto è un uom d'ottimo core.	**Zerlina:** Oh, my dear Masetto is such a generous man.
Don Giovanni: Oh anch'io, vedete! Voglio che siamo amici. Il vostro nome?	**Don Giovanni:** And be assured, I see it! Let's be friends. What is your name?
Zerlina: Zerlina.	**Zerlina;** Zerlina.
Don Giovanni: E il tuo?	**Don Giovanni:** *(to Masetto)* And yours?

Masetto: Masetto.	**Masetto:** Masetto.
Don Giovanni: O caro il mio Masetto! Cara la mia Zerlina! V'esibisco la mia protezione.	**Don Giovanni:** Ah my dear Masetto! My dear Zerlina! I am pleased to offer you my protection.

Don Giovanni looks for Leporello, who is among the peasant girls.

Leporello! Cosa fai lì, birbone?	Leporello, you knave! What are you doing over there?
Leporello: Anch'io, caro padrone, esibisco la mia protezione.	**Leporello:** I too, dear master, am offering my protection.
Don Giovanni: Presto, va con costor; nel mio palazzo conducili sul fatto: ordina ch'abbiano cioccolatta, caffè, vini, prosciutti; cerca divertir tutti, mostra loro il giardino, la galleria, le camere; in effetto fa che resti contento il mio Masetto. Hai capito?	**Don Giovanni:** Hurry, and take these happy people to my palace: order chocolate, coffee, wine, ham. Find a way to entertain them; show them the garden, the gallery, the rooms, and above all, make sure that my dear Masetto is happy. Do you understand?
Leporello: Ho capito. Andiam!	**Leporello:** I understand. *(to Masetto)* Let's go!
Masetto: Signore!	**Masetto:** Sir!
Don Giovanni: Cosa c'è?	**Don Giovanni:** What is it?
Masetto: La Zerlina senza me non può star.	**Masetto:** Zerlina can't stay here without me.
Leporello: In vostro loco ci sarà sua eccellenza; e saprà bene fare le vostre parti.	**Leporello:** *(to Masetto)* His excellency will take your place; he knows well how to play your part.
Don Giovanni: Oh, la Zerlina è in man d'un cavalier. Va pur, fra poco ella meco verrà.	**Don Giovanni:** Zerlina is in the care of a nobleman. Go then! She'll soon return with me.
Zerlina: Va! Non temere! Nelle mani son io d'un cavaliere.	**Zerlina:** Go! Don't worry! I am in the hands of a nobleman.

Masetto:
E per questo?

Masetto:
And for what reason?

Zerlina:
E per questo non c'è da dubitar

Zerlina:
Because there's no reason to worry.

Masetto:
Ed io, cospetto.

Masetto: *(trying to take Zerlina's hand)*
And what about me?

Don Giovanni:
Olà, finiam le dispute! Se subito senza altro replicar non te ne vai, Masetto, guarda ben, ti pentirai!

Don Giovanni: *(stepping between them)*
Now, the dispute is over! Masetto, be careful! If you don't leave immediately and without arguing, you'll regret it!

Masetto:
Ho capito, signor sì!
Chino il capo e me ne vo.
Già che piace a voi così,
altre repliche non fo.

Cavalier voi siete già.
Dubitar non posso affè;
me lo dice la bontà
che volete aver per me.

Bricconaccia, malandrina!
Fosti ognor la mia ruina!

Vengo, vengo!

Resta, resta.
È una cosa molto onesta!
Faccia il nostro cavaliere ancora te.

Masetto: *(dumbfounded)*
I understand sir, yes!
I just bow my head and go.
As you wish,
and no further argument.

You are indeed a cavalier.
I cannot doubt it.
You tell me how kind
you want to be with me.

(aside to Zerlina)
Little cheat! Viper!
You were born to be my ruin!

(Leporello forces Masetto away)
I'm coming, I'm coming!

(to Zerlina)
Stay, stay. It's quite prudent to trust him!
Let this nobleman also make a lady of you.

Leporello hurries Masetto into the tavern.

Don Giovanni:

Alfin siam liberati, Zerlinetta gentil, da quel scioccone. Che ne dite, mio ben, so far pulito?

Don Giovanni:
(trying to embrace Zerlina)
My gentle little Zerlina, at last we are free of that troublesome fellow. Tell me, my angel, didn't I handle it well?

Zerlina:
Signore, è mio marito!

Zerlina:
But Sir, he is my fiancé!

Don Giovanni:
Chi? Colui?
Vi par che un onest'uomo, un nobil cavalier, com'io mi vanto, possa soffrir che quel visetto d'oro, quel viso inzuccherato da un bifolcaccio vil sia strapazzato?

Don Giovanni:
Who! Him?
Do you think that an honest nobleman, a man of rank like me, can bear to see this such precious and sweet face snatched away by a plowman?

Zerlina:
Ma, signore, io gli diedi parola di sposarlo.

Zerlina:
But sir, I have promised to marry him.

Don Giovanni:
Tal parola non vale un zero. Voi non siete fatta per essere paesana; un altra sorte vi procuran quegli occhi bricconcelli, quei labretti sì belli, quelle dituccie candide e odorose, parmi toccar giuncata e fiutar rose.

Don Giovanni:
Such a promise means nothing. You were not born to be country wife. Those roguish eyes deserve another destiny. Those beautiful lips, those white-scented fingers, are like touching cream and sniffing roses.

Zerlina:
Ah! Non vorrei.

Zerlina:
Ah! I don't want to.

Don Giovanni:
Che non vorreste?

Don Giovanni:
What don't you want?

Zerlina:
Alfine ingannata restar. Io so che raro colle donne voi altri cavalieri siete onesti e sinceri.

Zerlina:
To be deceived in the end. I know that noblemen are seldom frank and honest with women.

Don Giovanni:
È un impostura della gente plebea! La nobilità ha dipinta negli occhi l'onestà. Orsù, non perdiam tempo; in questo istante io ti voglio sposar.

Don Giovanni:
It is a popular fiction of the common people! The nobility has honesty painted in its eyes. But let's not waste time: I want to marry you right away.

Zerlina:
Voi?

Zerlina:
You?

Don Giovanni:
Certo, io. Quel casinetto è mio: soli saremo e là, gioiello mio, ci sposeremo.

Don Giovanni:
(pointing to the country house) Certainly. That little house you see is mine. My treasure, there we can be alone, and there we will be married.

Là ci darem la mano,
là mi dirai di sì.
Vedi, non è lontano; partiam,
ben mio, da qui.

There, we'll take each other's hand,
and there, you will say yes.
Look, it isn't far.
Let's go, my love, let's go from here.

Zerlina:
(Vorrei e non vorrei,
mi trema un poco il cor.
Felice, è ver, sarei,
ma può burlarmi ancor!)

Zerlina:
(I would like to, and I wouldn't like to.
My heart is trembling a little.
It's true, I'd be happy,
unless this nobleman deceives me!)

Don Giovanni:
Vieni, mio bel diletto!

Don Giovanni:
Come, my beautiful treasure!

Zerlina:
(Mi fa pietà Masetto!)

Zerlina:
(I feel sorry for Masetto!)

Don Giovanni:
Io cangierò tua sorte!

Don Giovanni:
I will change your fate!

Zerlina:
Presto, non son più forte!

Zerlina:
I feel myself weakening so quickly!

Don Giovanni:
Vieni, vieni! Andiam! Andiam!

Don Giovanni:
Come, come! Let's go! Let's go!

Zerlina:
Andiam!

Zerlina:
Let's go!

A due:
Andiam, andiam, mio bene
a ristorar le pene
s'un innocente amor!

Together:
Let's go, let's go, my love
to share the pleasure
of innocence and love!

Donna Elvira has been watching Don Giovanni and Zerlina.
As Don Giovanni and Zerlina walk toward the little house (casino),
Donna Elvira blocks their passage.

Donna Elvira:
Fermati, scellerato! Il ciel mi fece udir le tue perfidie!
Io sono a tempo di salvar questa misera innocente dal tuo barbaro artiglio!

Donna Elvira:
Stop, scoundrel! Heaven made me hear your perfidious behavior!
I have arrived just in time to save this poor innocent girl from your barbaric clutches!

Zerlina:
Meschina! Cosa sento!

Zerlina:
Oh, my! What I am hearing!

Don Giovanni:
(Amor, consiglio!)
Idol mio, non vedete ch'io voglio divertirmi?

Don Giovanni:
(Cupid, advise me!) *(softly to Elvira)*
My love, don't you see that I am amusing myself?

Donna Elvira:
Divertirti, è vero? Divertirti, io so, crudele, come tu ti diverti.

Donna Elvira:
Amusing yourself? Yes, cruel man, I know too well how you amuse yourself.

Zerlina:
Ma, signor cavaliere, è ver quel ch'ella dice?

Zerlina: *(anxiously to Don Giovanni)*
But, my lord, is this lady telling the truth?

Don Giovanni:
La povera infelice è di me innamorata, e per pietà deggio fingere amore, ch'io son, per mia disgrazia, uom di buon cuore.

Don Giovanni: *(softly to Zerlina)*
The poor unhappy women is in love with me, and out of pity I pretend to love her. That is my misfortune. I am so kind-hearted.

After Don Giovanni departs, Donna Elvira admonishes Zerlina.

Donna Elvira:
Ah, fuggi il traditor!
Non lo lasciar più dir!
Il labbro è mentitor,
fallace il ciglio!

Da' miei tormenti impara
a creder a quel cor,
e nasca il tuo timor
dal mio periglio!

Donna Elvira:
Escape from this traitor!
Don't let him say anything more!
His words are all lies,
and deception is in his eyes!

Learn from my torment,
and believe my heart.
And let my misfortune
arouse your fear!

Donna Elvira leads Zerlina away.

Don Giovanni:
Mi par ch'oggi il demonio si diverta d'opporsi a miei piacevoli progressi vanno mal tutti quanti.

Don Giovanni:
It seems that today the devil enjoys himself by opposing my pursuit of pleasures. All my schemes are going badly.

Don Octavio and Donna Anna appear.

Don Ottavio:
Ah! Ch'ora, idolo mio, son vani i pianti, di vendetta si parli!
Oh, Don Giovanni!

Don Octavio:
Dearest Donna Anna, those tears are in vain, when you speak only of revenge!
Oh, Don Giovanni!

Don Giovanni:
(Mancava questo intoppo!)

Don Giovanni:
(And now this unfortunate encounter!)

Donna Anna:
Signore, a tempo vi ritroviam.
Avete core?
Avete anima generosa?

Donna Anna:
Sir, we have found you at an opportune time. Do you have a good heart?
Do you have a generous soul?

Don Giovanni:
(Sta a vedere che il diavolo gli ha detto qualche cosa.)
Che domanda! Perchè?

Don Giovanni:
(I wonder whether the devil has told her something.) What a question, Madame!
Why do you ask it?

Donna Anna:
Bisogno abbiamo della vostra amicizia.

Donna Anna:
We have need of your friendship.

Don Giovanni:
(Mi torna il fiato in corpo.)
Comandate. I congiunti, i parenti, questa man, questo ferro, i beni, il sangue spenderò per servirvi.
Ma voi, bella Donn'Anna, perchè così piangete? Il crudele chi fu che osò la calma turbar del viver vostro?

Don Giovanni:
(I breathe again.)
Command me. My kinsmen, my relations, this arm, my sword, my wealth, my blood: all are at your service. But you, beautiful Donna Anna, why are you crying? Who is the wretch who has dared to disturb your peaceful life?

Donna Elvira enters.

Donna Elvira:
Ah, ti ritrovo ancor, perfido mostro! Non ti fidar, o misera, di quel ribaldo cor! Me già tradì quel barbaro, te vuol tradir ancor.

Donna Elvira: *(to Don Giovanni)*
Ah, I find you again, you perfidious monster! (to *Donna Anna)* Sad lady, do not confide in this rogue! This barbarian has already betrayed me, and he wants to betray you too.

Donna Anna e Don Ottavio:
(Cieli, che aspetto nobile!
Che dolce maestà! Il suo pallor, le lagrime m'empiono di pietà.)

Donna Anna and Don Octavio:
(Heavens, what a noble bearing she has!
What gentle grace! Her ashen face and her tears, fill me with pity.)

Don Giovanni:
La povera ragazza è pazza, amici miei!
Lasciatemi con lei, forse si calmerà!

Don Giovanni: *(trying to draw Elvira away)*
My friends, this poor young woman is crazy! Leave her with me, and perhaps I can calm her down!

Donna Elvira:
Ah! Non credete al perfido!

Donna Elvira:
Don't believe this perfidious man!

Don Giovanni:
È pazza, non badate!

Don Giovanni:
She's crazy, don't listen to her!

Donna Elvira:
Restate ancor, restate!

Donna Elvira:
Stay, stay!

Donna Anna e Don Ottavio:
A chi si crederà?

Donna Anna and Don Octavio:
Who should we believe?

Donna Anna, Don Ottavio, Don Giovanni:
Certo moto d'ignoto tormento
dentro l'alma girare mi sento;
Che mi dice, per quell'infelice.
Cento cose che intender non sa!

Donna Anna, Don Octavio, Don Giovanni:
I have a mysterious feeling
turning in my soul;
it tells me that she is an unhappy woman.
So many impossible things to understand!

Donna Elvira:
Sdegno, rabbia, dispetto, spavento.
Dentro l'alma girare mi sento,
che mi dice, di quel traditore.
Cento cose che intender non sa!

Donna Elvira:
I am fearful, scornful and angry
I have a mysterious feeling turning in my
soul; it tells me about this traitor.
So many impossible things to understand!

Don Ottavio:
(Io di qua non vado via se non so com'è l'affar!)

Don Octavio:
(I will not leave from here until I learn the truth of this mystery!)

Donna Anna:
Non ha l'aria di pazzia il suo tratto, il suo parlar.

Donna Anna:
(She doesn't look or sound crazy to me.)

Don Giovanni:
(Se m'en vado, si potrìa qualche cosa sospettar.)

Don Giovanni:
(If I go now, they'll become suspicious.)

Donna Elvira:
Da quel ceffo si dovrìa la ner'alma giudicar.

Donna Elvira: *(to Anna and Octavio)*
The dark soul of that beast should be judged.

Don Ottavio:
Dunque quella?

Don Octavio: *(to Don Giovanni)*
What does she say?

Don Giovanni:
È pazzarella!

Don Giovanni:
She's a little crazy!

Donna Anna:
Dunque quegli?

Donna Anna: *(to Elvira)*
And what do you say?

Donna Elvira:
È un traditore.

Donna Elvira:
He is a traitor.

Don Giovanni:
Infelice!

Don Giovanni:
Unhappy woman!

Donna Elvira:
Mentitore!

Donna Elvira:
Liar!

Donna Anna e Don Ottavio:
Incomincio a dubitar.

Donna Anna and Don Octavio:
I'm beginning to have doubts.

Don Giovanni:
Zitto, zitto, che la gente
si raduna a noi d'intorno;
siate un poco più prudente,
vi farete criticar.

Don Giovanni: *(aside to Elvira)*
Quiet, people are coming
and gathering all around,
be a little more prudent,
or else you'll be criticized.

Donna Elvira:
Non sperarlo, o scellerato,
ho perduta la prudenza;
le tue colpe ed il mio stato
voglio a tutti palesar.

Donna Elvira: *(loudly to Don Giovanni)*
Don't count on it, you scoundrel,
I have lost prudence;
I want to reveal to everyone
your sins and my sad fate.

Donna Anna e Don Ottavio:
Quegli accenti sì sommessi,
quel cangiarsi di colore,
son indizi troppo espressi.
Che mi fan determinar.

Donna Anna and Don Octavio:
He's altered his manner,
and his pallor has changed.
His expression makes me
see the truth.

Don Giovanni leads Elvira away, and then returns alone.

Don Giovanni:
Povera sventurata!
I passi suoi voglio seguir; non voglio che
faccia un precipizio.

Perdonate, bellissima Donn'Anna!
Se servirvi poss'io, in mia casa v'aspetto.
Amici, addio!

Don Giovanni:
Poor woman!
I must follow her because I don't want her
to do something desperate.

Forgive me, fair Donna Anna;
if I can serve you, I await you at my home.
Friends, farewell!

Don Giovanni departs hastily.

Donna Anna:
Don Ottavio! Son morta!

Donna Anna: *(in extreme agitation)*
Don Octavio! I'm petrified!

Don Ottavio:
Cosa è stato?

Don Octavio:
What is it?

Donna Anna:
Per pietà, soccorretemi!

Donna Anna:
For pity's sake, help me!

Don Ottavio:
Mio bene, fate coraggio!

Don Octavio:
My love, have courage!

Donna Anna:
Oh Dei! Quegli è il carnefice del padre mio!

Donna Anna:
Oh gods! He is the murderer of my father!

Don Ottavio:
Che dite?

Donna Anna:
Non dubitate più. Gli ultimi accenti che l'empio proferì, tutta la voce richiamar nel cór mio di quell'indegno che nel mio appartamento.

Don Ottavio:
O ciel! Possibile che sotto il sacro manto d'amicizia ma come fu, narratemi lo strano avvenimento.

Donna Anna:
Era già alquanto avanzata la notte,
quando nelle mie stanze, ove soletta
mi trovai per sventura, entrar io vidi,
in un mantello avvolto, un uom che al
primo istante avea preso per voi.
Ma riconobbi poi che un inganno era il mio!

Don Ottavio:
Stelle! Seguite!

Donna Anna:
Tacito a me s'appresa e mi vuole
abbracciar;
sciogliermi cerco, ei più mi stringe;
io grido; non viene alcun:
con una mano cerca d'impedire la voce,
e coll'altra m'afferra stretta così,
che già mi credo vinta.

Don Ottavio:
Perfido! Alfin?

Donna Anna:
Alfine il duol, l'orrore dell'infame attentato accrebbe sì la lena mia, che a forza di svincolarmi, torcermi e piegarmi, da lui mi sciolsi!

Don Ottavio:
Ohimè! Respiro!

Donna Anna:
Allora rinforzo i stridi miei, chiamo soccorso; fugge il fellon;

Don Octavio:
What are you saying?

Donna Anna:
I know for sure. The intonation of his voice reminds me of that contemptible villain who barged into my apartment.

Don Octavio:
Heavens! Can this be possible under the sacred guise of friendship? But tell me what happened.

Donna Anna: *(extremely emotional)*
It was already late at night,
when I was alone in my rooms.
I saw someone enter, wrapped in a cloak,
a man, who at first I took for you.
But then I realized that I'd made a mistake!

Don Octavio: *(agitated)*
The wretch! Continue!

Donna Anna:
He approached me silently and then wanted
to kiss me.
I tried to free myself and shouted, but no
one came.
He covered my mouth with one hand,
and with the other grasped me so forcibly,
that I thought I was finished.

Don Octavio:
That villain! And then?

Donna Anna:
Finally my grief and despair strengthened me against this infamous creature. After struggling, twisting and turning, I freed myself and escaped from him.

Don Octavio:
I can breathe again!

Donna Anna:
Then I called for help, screaming louder as the villain fled.

arditamente il seguo fin nella strada per fermarlo,
e sono assalitrice ed assalita:
il padre v'accorre, vuol conoscerlo e l'indegno
che del povero vecchio era più forte,
compiè il misfatto suo col dargli morte!

I boldly followed him into the street to stop him; as such, I became the assailant who was once the assailed.
My father ran to my aid and wanted to find out who it was.
But the old man was weaker than his foe;
he was overpowered and met his doom!

Andante
DONNA ANNA

Or sai chi l'onore
aprire a me volse,
chi fu il traditore
che il padre mi tolse.
Vendetta ti chieggo,
la chiede il tuo cor!

I now know who it was who
tried to steal my honor,
and who the traitor was
who took my father from me.
It is vengeance I ask.
And your heart asks it too!

Rammenta la piaga
del misero seno,
rimira di sangue.
coperto il terreno.
Se l'ira in te langue
d'un giusto furor.

Remember the wound
in his poor breast,
and remember his blood
covering the ground,
if your anguish for a just revenge
should diminish.

Donna Anna departs.

Don Ottavio:
Come mai creder deggio,
di sì nero delitto capace un cavaliere!
Ah! Di scoprire il vero ogni mezzo si cerchi.
Io sento in petto
e di sposo e d'amico il dover che mi parla:
disingannarla voglio, o vendicarla!

Don Octavio:
How can one believe that this cavalier was capable of such a terrible crime!
Ah! I will use every means to discover the truth. I feel my heart speaking to me like her husband and friend. I wish to free her from deception and avenge her!

DON OTTAVIO

Dalla sua pace la mia dipende;
quel che a lei piace vita mi rende,
quel che le incresce morte mi dà.
S'ella sospira, sospiro anch'io;
è mia quell'ira, quel pianto è mio;
e non ho bene, s'ella non l'ha!

My peace depends on her peace.
Whatever pleases her gives me joy,
what displeases her brings me death.
If she sighs, I also sigh,
because her anger is mine, and her tears are mine. I am not content if she is not content!

Don Octavio exits.

Leporello enters from the tavern, Don Giovanni from his palace.

Leporello:
Io deggio ad ogni patto per sempre abbandonar questo bel matto.
Eccolo qui: guardate con qual indifferenza se ne viene!

Leporello:
Whatever the consequence may be, I must leave this mad rake forever.
Here he comes. Look at his indifferent air!

Don Giovanni:
Oh, Leporello mio! Va tutto bene?

Don Giovanni:
My Leporello! Does all go well?

Leporello:
Don Giovannino mio! Va tutto male!

Leporello:
My little Don Giovanni! All goes badly!

Don Giovanni:
Come va tutto male?

Don Giovanni:
Why badly?

Leporello:
Vado a casa, come voi m'ordinaste, con tutta quella gente.

Leporello:
As you ordered me, I went to the house with all those people.

Don Giovanni:
Bravo!

Don Giovanni:
Very good!

Leporello:
A forza di chiacchiere, di vezzi e di bugie, ch'ho imparato sì bene a star con voi, cerco d'intrattenerli.

Leporello:
I used lots of chatter and the usual deceptions that I have learned so well from you in my attempt to keep them there.

Don Giovanni:
Bravo!

Don Giovanni:
Very good!

Leporello:
Dico mille cose a Masetto per placarlo, per trargli dal pensier la gelosia.

Leporello:
I said a thousand things to Masetto to pacify him and erase any of his jealous thoughts.

Don Giovanni:
Bravo! In coscienza mia!

Don Giovanni:
Very good! A conscience like mine!

Leporello:
Faccio che bevano e gli uomini e le donne; son già mezzo ubbriachi, altri canta, altri scherza, altri seguita a ber. In sul più bello, chi credete che capiti?

Leporello:
I had the men and women drinking; they were already half drunk. Some were singing, some joking, and others continued to drink. Just as all was going well, who do you think arrived?

Don Giovanni:
Zerlina!.

Don Giovanni:
Zerlina!

Leporello:
Bravo! E con lei chi viene?

Leporello:
Right! And who do you think was with her?

Don Giovanni:
Donna Elvira!

Don Giovanni:
Donna Elvira!

Leporello:
Bravo! E disse di voi?

Leporello:
Right! Did she tell you?

Don Giovanni:
Tutto quel mal che in bocca le venìa.

Don Giovanni:
All the evil she could imagine came from her lips!

Leporello:
Bravo, in coscienza mia!

Leporello:
True, upon my word!

Don Giovanni:
E tu, cosa facesti?

Don Giovanni:
And what did you do?

Leporello:
Tacqui.

Leporello:
Nothing.

Don Giovanni:
Ed ella?

Don Giovanni:
And she?

Leporello:
Seguì a gridar.

Leporello:
Continued to shout.

Don Giovanni:
E tu?

Don Giovanni:
And you?

Leporello:
Quando mi parve che già fosse sfogata, dolcemente fuor dell'orto la trassì, e con bell'arte chiusa la porta a chiave io di là mi cavai, e sulla via soletta la lasciai.

Leporello:
When she appeared to be exhausted, I gently led her out of the garden, and then adroitly closed the door, locked it and rode off. I left her standing alone in the street.

Don Giovanni:
Bravo! Bravo, arci bravo!
L'affar non può andar meglio.
Incominciasti, io saprò terminar.
Troppo mi premono queste contadinotte;
le voglio divertir finchè vien notte.

Don Giovanni:
Superb! Superb, absolutely perfect! The affair could not have gone better. What you began, I will finish. These pretty country girls bewitch me. I want to amuse them until nightfall.

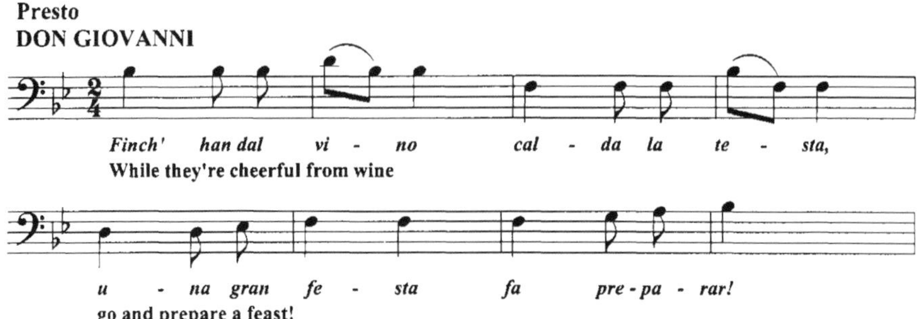

Finch'han dal vino calda la testa una gran festa fa preparar! Se trovi in piazza qualche ragazza, teco ancor quella cerca menar.	While they're cheerful from wine go and prepare a feast! If you find some girl in the plaza, bring her with you.
Senza alcun ordine la danza sia, chi il minuetto, chi la follia, chi l'alemanna farai ballar!	Without further ado, get the dance going. Make them dance, a minuet, a frolic, or the allemande!
Ed io frattanto dall'altro canto con questa e quella vo' amoreggiar. Ah! La mia lista doman mattina d'una decina devi aumentar!	And I'll be among them, making love with this one or that one. Tomorrow morning, my list must increase by a dozen!

Leporello goes into the tavern to fetch the peasants. Don Giovanni rushes into his palace.

ACT I - Scene 4

A garden. On one side, Don Giovanni's palace; on the other, a pavilion.

Zerlina: Masetto, senti un po'! Masetto, dico!	**Zerlina:** Masetto, listen a moment to what I have to say!
Masetto: Non mi toccar!	**Masetto:** Don't touch me!
Zerlina: Perchè?	**Zerlina:** Why?
Masetto: Perchè mi chiedi? Perfida! Il tocco sopportar dovrei d'una mano infedele?	**Masetto:** You don't know why? Betrayer! Must I touch your unfaithful hand?
Zerlina: Ah no, taci, crudele, io non merito da te tal trattamento.	**Zerlina:** Oh no. You're cruel. I don't deserve such treatment.

Masetto:
Come? Ed hai l'ardimento di scusarti?
Star solo con un uom, abbandonarmi il dì delle mie nozze!
Porre in fronte a un villano d'onore questa marca d'infamia!
Ah, se non fosse, se non fosse lo scandalo, vorrei...

Masetto:
Why? Do you have the audacity to make excuses? You were alone with a man and abandoned me on our wedding day!
To do this with such a villain is a mark of disgrace!
And if it were not because I fear a scandal, I would...

Zerlina:
Ma se colpa io non ho, ma se da lui ingannata rimasi; e poi, che temi?
Tranquillati, mia vita; non mi toccò la punta della dita.
Non me lo credi? Ingrato!
Vien qui, sfogati, ammazzami, fa tutto di me quel che ti piace, ma poi, Masetto mio, ma poi fa pace.

Zerlina:
He tried to deceive me, but I did nothing wrong. So what do you fear?
Be calm, he didn't touch the tip of my finger. Don't you believe me?
You're so ungrateful! Come here!
Vent your anger, kill me, do what you want to me, but then, my dear Masetto, but then let's make peace.

Batti, batti, o bel Masetto,
la tua povera Zerlina;
Starò qui come agnellina
le tue botte ad aspettar.
Lascerò straziarmi il crine,
lascerò cavarmi gli occhi, e le care tue manine lieta poi saprò baciar.

Beat me, beat me, dear Masetto,
beat your poor Zerlina.
I'll be like a patient lamb
and await your flogging.
I'll let you tear out my hair, I'll let you dig out my eyes, and then I'll happily kiss those dear hands of yours.

Ah, lo vedo, non hai core!
Pace, pace, o vita mia,
in contento ed allegria
notte e dì vogliam passar,
Sì, notte e dì vogliam passar.

Oh, I see you haven't the heart!
Peace, peace, my love,
Let's spend night and day
in peace and contentment Yes, in peace and contentment.

Masetto:
Guarda un po' come seppe questa strega sedurmi! Siamo pure i deboli di testa!

Masetto:
Look how this enchantress has seduced me!
We men must all have weak minds!

Don Giovanni:
Sia preparato tutto a una gran festa.

Don Giovanni: *(from inside)*
Prepare a grand feast for everyone.

Zerlina:
Ah Masetto, Masetto, odi la voce del monsù cavaliere!

Zerlina: *(frightened)*
Oh, Masetto, Masetto, it's the voice of the cavalier!

Masetto:
Ebben, che c'è?

Masetto:
Well, what of that?

Zerlina:
Verrà!

Zerlina:
He'll be coming here!

Masetto:
Lascia che venga.

Masetto:
Let him come.

Zerlina:
Ah, se vi fosse un buco da fuggir!

Zerlina:
Oh, if only there was a place to hide from him!

Masetto:
Di cosa temi?
Perché diventi pallida?
Ah, capisco! Capisco, bricconcella,
hai timor ch'io comprenda com'è tra voi passata la faccenda.

Presto, presto, pria ch'ei venga,
por mi vo' da qualche lato;
c'è una nicchia qui celato, cheto cheto mi vo' star.

Masetto:
What are you afraid of?
Why do you turn pale?
Ah, I understand! I understand, you little cheat, you're afraid that I'll find out what took place between the both of you.

Quickly, quickly, before he comes. I'll move aside.
There's a nook. I'll stay there and hide quietly.

Zerlina:
Senti, senti, dove vai? Ah, non t'asconder, o Masetto! Se ti trova, poveretto, tu non sai quel che può far.

Zerlina:
Listen, listen, where are you going?
Masetto, don't hide! If he finds you, my poor fellow, you don't know what he might do.

Masetto:
Faccia, dica quel che vuole.

Masetto:
Let him say or do what he wishes.

Zerlina:
Ah, non giovan le parole!

Zerlina:
Words are just useless!

Masetto:
Parla forte, e qui t'arresta!

Masetto;
Speak louder so I can hear you!

Zerlina:
Che capriccio hai nella testa?

Zerlina:
What nonsense do you have in your mind?

Masetto:(
Capirò se m'è fedele, e in qual modo andò l'affar!)

Masetto:
(I will learn whether she is faithful, and just how far their intrigue went!)

Zerlina:
(Quell'ingrato, quel crudele, oggi vuol precipitar.)

Zerlina:
(How cruel and ungrateful! He's looking for trouble today.)

Masetto hides in the arbor as Don Giovanni arrives.

Don Giovanni:
Sù! Svegliatevi da bravi!
Sù! Coraggio, o buona gente!
Vogliam star allegramente,
vogliam ridere e scherzar.

Don Giovanni: *(to the peasants)*
Come on! Get up and enjoy yourselves!
Come! Be hearty good people!
Let's be happy!
Let's laugh and play!

Alla stanza, della danza
conducete tutti quanti,
ed a tutti in abbondanza
gran rifreschi fate dar!

(to the servants)
Take all of them to the hall
for dancing,
and give them all
plenty of great refreshments!

Coro:
Sù! Svegliatevi da bravi!

Chorus of peasants:
Come on! Get up and enjoy yourselves!

After the peasants leave, Zerlina tries to hide herself among the trees.

Zerlina:
Tra quest'arbori celata, si può dar che non mi veda.

Zerlina:
Perhaps he won't see me if I am concealed among these trees.

Don Giovanni:
Zerlinetta, mia garbata, t'ho già visto, non scappar!

Don Giovanni:
My sweet Zerlina, I now see you, and you cannot escape!

Zerlina:
Ah lasciatemi andar via!

Zerlina:
Let me go away!

Don Giovanni:
No, no, resta, gioia mia!

Don Giovanni:
No, stay, my angel!

Zerlina:
Se pietade avete in core!

Zerlina:
If you have one bit of pity in your heart!

Don Giovanni:
Sì, ben mio! Son tutto amore. Vieni un poco, in questo loco fortunata io ti vo' far!

Don Giovanni:
Yes, my dearest! I'm all love. Come with me, it will be worthwhile for you!

Zerlina:
(Ah, s'ei vede il sposo mio, so ben io quel che può far!)

Zerlina:
(Oh, if my jealous fiancé sees him, I know well what he could do!)

Don Giovanni discovers the hiding Masetto.

Don Giovanni:
Masetto?

Don Giovanni:
Masetto?

Masetto:
Sì, Masetto!

Masetto:
Yes, Masetto!

Don Giovanni:
E chiuso là, perchè? La bella tua Zerlina non può, la poverina, più star senza di te.

Don Giovanni:
And why are you hiding there? Your pretty Zerlina, poor thing, can no longer be without you.

Masetto:
Capisco, sì signore.

Masetto: *(with irony)*
I understand, my lord.

Don Giovanni:
Adesso fate core. I suonatori udite? Venite ormai con me!

Don Giovanni:
Come, be strong. Do you hear the musicians? Now come with me!

Zerlina e Masetto:
Sì, sì, facciamo core, ad a ballar cogli altri. Andiamo tutti tre!

Zerlina and Masetto:
Yes, yes, let's all capture the spirit, and dance with the others. Let's all three go together!

Don Giovanni, Zerlina and Masetto leave for the ball.

As evening descends. Don Octavio, Donna Anna and Donna Elvira arrive; all are masked.

Donna Elvira:
Bisogna aver coraggio, o cari amici miei, e i suoi misfatti rei scoprir potremo allor.

Donna Elvira:
We must be courageous, my dear friends, and then we can uncover his wicked deeds.

Don Ottavio:
L'amica dice bene, coraggio aver conviene; Discaccia, o vita mia, l'affanno ed il timor!

Don Octavio: *(to Donna Anna).*
Our friend speaks wisely-, we must be righteous. Oh my dearest, your fear and terror will soon end!

Donna Anna:
Il passo è periglioso, può nascer qualche imbroglio.
Temo pel caro sposo,
e per voi temo ancor!

Donna Anna:
This action is dangerous, and can lead to a squabble.
I fear for my beloved fiancé,
(to Donna Elvira) and for you as well!

Leporello points out the masqueraders to Don Giovanni.

Leporello:
Signor, guardate un poco, che maschere galanti!

Leporello:
Sir, take a moment and look at the gallant masqueraders!

Don Giovanni:
Falle passar avanti, di' che ci fanno onor!

Don Giovanni:
Invite them in, and tell them we would be honored!

Donna Anna, Donna Elvira e Don Ottavio:
(Al volto ed alla voce si scopre il traditore!)

Donna Anna, Donna Elvira and Don Octavio:
(The traitor reveals himself by his bearing and his voice!)

Leporello:
Zì, zì! Signore maschere!

Leporello:
Psst, psst! Noble masqueraders!

Donna Anna e Donna Elvira:
Via, rispondete.

Donna Anna, Donna Elvira: *(to Octavio)*
Go, you respond to him.

Leporello:
Signore maschere!

Leporello:
Noble masqueraders!

Don Ottavio:
Cosa chiedete?

Don Octavio:
What are you asking for?

Leporello:
Al ballo, se vi piace, v'invita il mio signor.

Leporello:
My lord invites you, if you would, to join the ball.

Don Ottavio:
Grazie di tanto onore!
Andiam, compagne belle.

Don Octavio:
Thank you for such an honor!
Let's go, beautiful companions.

Leporello:
(L'amico anche su quelle prova farà d'amor!)

Leporello:
(My lord will quickly try to make love to the women!)

Leporello enters the palace.

Donna Anna e Don Ottavio:
Protegga il giusto cielo il zelo del mio cor!

Donna Anna and Don Octavio:
May the just heavens protect the fierceness in my heart!

Donna Elvira:
Vendichi il giusto cielo il mio tradito amor!

Donna Elvira:
May the just heavens avenge my betrayed love!

The three masqueraders enter the palace.

ACT I - Scene 5

The brilliantly illuminated ballroom of Don Giovanni's palace.

Don Giovanni:
Riposate, vezzose ragazze.

Don Giovanni:
(ushering some young girls to seats)
Pretty girls, rest from your dancing.

Leporello:
Rinfrescatevi, bei giovinotti!

Leporello:
Good men, some refreshments!

Don Giovanni e Leporello:
Tornerete a far presto le pazze, tornerete a scherzar e ballar!

Don Giovanni and Leporello:
You'll soon be returning to your passions of playing and dancing!

Don Giovanni:
Ehi! Caffè!

Don Giovanni:
Hey! Some coffee!

Leporello:
Cioccolata!

Leporello:
Some chocolate!

Masetto:
Ah, Zerlina, giudizio!

Masetto: *(anxiously holding Zerlina)*
Zerlina, be prudent!

Don Giovanni:
Sorbetti!

Don Giovanni:
Sherbet!

Leporello:
Confetti!

Leporello:
Some sweets!

Masetto:
Ah, Zerlina, giudizio!

Masetto:
Zerlina, be prudent!

Zerlina e Masetto:
(Troppo dolce comincia la scena; in amaro potrìa terminar!)

Zerlina and Masetto:
(The scene begins so sweetly, but may end bitterly!)

Don Giovanni:
Sei pur vaga, brillante Zerlina!

Don Giovanni:
Lovely Zerlina, you are indeed charming!

Zerlina:
Sua bontà!

Zerlina:
Your lordship is very polite!

Masetto:
(La briccona fa festa!)

Masetto: *(aside furiously).*
(The rascal is enjoying herself!)

Leporello:
Sei pur cara, Gionnotta, Sandrina.

Leporello: *(amongst the girls)*
How pretty you are, Giannotta, Sandrina!

Masetto:
(Tocca pur, che ti cada la testa!)

Masetto:
(Touch her and your head will fall!)

Zerlina:
(Quel Masetto mi par stralunato, brutto, brutto si fa quest'affar!)

Zerlina: *(looking at Masetto)*
(That Masetto has gone mad; he's in an awful predicament!)

Don Giovanni e Leporello:
(Quel Masetto mi par stralunato,
qui bisogna cervello adoprar.)

Don Giovanni and Leporello:
(That Masetto seems a little crazy.
I must use all my skill to win her.)

The masqueraders enter the ballroom.

Leporello: Venite pur avanti, vezzose mascherette!	**Leporello:** Come forward, charming masqueraders!
Don Giovanni: È aperto a tutti quanti. Viva la libertà!	**Don Giovanni:** My house is open to everyone. Long live liberty!
Donna Anna, Donna Elvira e Don Ottavio: Siam grati a tanti segni di generosità!	**Donna Anna, Donna Elvira and Don Octavio:** We are grateful for those gestures of hospitality!
Tutti: Viva la libertà!	**All:** Long live liberty!
Don Giovanni: Ricominciate il suono! Tu accoppia i ballerini!	**Don Giovanni:** Go on with the music! *(to Leporello)* You pair the dancers!

Don Giovanni addresses the masqueraders.

Da bravi, via ballate!	Good people, come and dance!

Don Giovanni begins to dance with Zerlina.

Donna Elvira: (Quella è la contadina.)	**Donna Elvira:** *(to Donna Anna pointing out Zerlina)* (That is the country girl.)
Donna Anna: (Io moro!)	**Donna Anna:** *(to Don Octavio)* (I feel like I am dying!)
Don Ottavio: (Simulate!)	**Don Octavio:** *(to Donna Anna)* (Hide your feelings!)
Don Giovanni e Leporello: Va bene in verità!	**Don Giovanni and Leporello:** All is going well!
Masetto: Va bene in verità!	**Masetto:** *(ironically)* Yes, everything is going well!
Don Giovanni: A bada tièn Masetto.	**Don Giovanni:** *(to Leporello)* Take good care of Masetto.
Leporello: Non balli, poveretto! Vien quà, Masetto caro, facciam quel ch'altri fa.	**Leporello:** *(to Masetto)* You're not dancing! Come here, my friend Masetto, and let us do as the others.

Don Giovanni:
Il tuo compagno io sono. Zerlina vien pur qua!

Don Giovanni: (to *Zerlina)*
I am your partner. Zerlina come with me!
(Leporello dances with Masetto)

Leporello:
Eh, balla, amico mio!

Leporello:
Hey, dance my friend!

Masetto:
No!

Masetto:
No!

Leporello:
Sì! Caro Masetto!

Leporello:
Yes! Dear Masetto!

Masetto:
No, no, ballar non voglio!

Masetto:
No, no, I don't want to dance!

Donna Anna:
Resister non poss'io!

Donna Anna:
I can no longer endure!

Donna Elvira e Don Ottavio:
Fingete per pietà!

Donna Elvira and Don Octavio:
Pretend, for pity's sake!

Don Giovanni places his arm about Zerlina's waist and draws her toward a door.

Don Giovanni:
Vieni con me, vita mia!

Don Giovanni:
Come with me, my love!

Masetto:
Lasciami! Ah no! Zerlina!

Masetto: *(to Leporello)*
Leave me alone! Oh no! Zerlina!

Zerlina:
Oh Numi! Son tradita!

Zerlina:
Oh, Heavens I'm betrayed!

Don Giovanni forces Zerlina into the room.

Leporello:
Qui nasce una ruina.

Leporello:
Another disaster is being born.

Donna Anna, Donna Elvira e Don Ottavio:
L'iniquo da se stesso nel laccio se ne va!

Donna Anna, Donna Elvira and Don Octavio:
The vile intriguer will be caught in his own trap!

Zerlina:
Gente, aiuto! Aiuto! Gente!

Zerlina: *(from within the room)*
Help me! Someone help me!

Donna Anna, Donna Elvira e Don Ottavio:
Soccorriamo l'innocente!

Donna Anna, Donna Elvira e Don Octavio:
Let's save the innocent girl!

Masetto:
Ah, Zerlina!

Masetto:
Oh, Zerlina!

Zerlina:
Scellerato!

Zerlina: *(from within)*
Evil man!

Donna Anna, Donna Elvira e Don Ottavio:
Ora grida da quel lato!
Ah gettiamo giù la porta!

Donna Anna, Donna Elvira and Don Octavio:
The shout comes from that side!
Let's break down the door!

Zerlina:
Soccorretemi! O son morta!

Zerlina: *(from within)*
Save me, or I'll die!

Donna Anna, Donna Elvira, Don Ottavio e Masetto:
Siam qui noi per tua difesa!

Donna Anna, Donna Elvira and Don Octavio:
We're here to defend you!

They break open the door. Don Giovanni emerges holding Leporello by the arm.

Don Giovanni:
Ecco il birbo che t'ha offesa! Ma da me la pena avrà! Mori, iniquo!

Don Giovanni:
Here is the culprit who offended you! But my hand shall punish him! Die, criminal!

Leporello:
Ah, cosa fate?

Leporello:
What are you doing?

Don Giovanni:
Mori, dico!

Don Giovanni:
Die, criminal!

Don Ottavio:
Nol sperate.

Don Octavio:
(holding a pistol to Giovanni)
Don't have hope that you can escape.

Donna Anna, Donna Elvira e Don Ottavio:
(L'empio crede con tal frode di nasconder l'empietà!)

Donna Anna, Donna Elvira and Don Octavio: *(all unmask)*
(The villain thinks he can hide his wickedness from us!)

Don Giovanni:
Donna Elvira?

Don Giovanni:
Donna Elvira?

Donna Elvira:
Sì, malvagio!

Donna Elvira:
Yes, you false one!

Don Giovanni:
Don Ottavio?

Don Giovanni:
Don Octavio?

Don Ottavio:
Sì, signore!

Don Octavio:
Yes, Signor!

Don Giovanni:
Ah, credete.

Don Giovanni:
Unbelievable.

Donna Anna:
Traditore!

Donna Anna:
You traitor!

Donna Anna, Donna Elvira e Don Ottavio:
Traditore! Traditore! Tutto già si sa!

Donna Anna, Donna Elvira and Don Octavio:
Traitor! Traitor! Everything is now known!

They approach Don Giovanni threateningly.

Trema, trema, o scellerato!

Tremble, tremble, scoundrel!

Zerlina:
Saprà tosto il mondo intero
il misfatto orrendo e nero
la tua fiera crudeltà!

Zerlina:
My head is confused
from your dark and horrible deeds
and your fierce cruelty!

Tutti:
Odi il tuon della vendetta,
che ti fischia intorno intorno;
Sul tuo capo in questo giorno
il suo fulmine cadrà!

All: *(except Giovanni and Leporello)*
Hear the thunder of vengeance,
that roars all around.
On this day, a thunderbolt
will fall on his head!

Don Giovanni e Leporello:
È confusa la mia testa!
Non sa più quel ch'ei si faccia
È un orribile tempesta minacciando,
o Dio, lo va!

Don Giovanni and Leporello:
My head is confused!
I do not know what I should do.
It is a horrible menacing storm
that God has wrought!

Ma non manca in lui coraggio,
non si perde o si confonde.
Se cadesse ancora il mondo,
nulla mai temer lo fa!

But my courage doesn't fail me,
I'm not lost or confused.
If the world might yet fall apart,
there is nothing I fear!

Don Giovanni seizes Leporello. Both push their way through the crowd and escape.

END OF ACT I

ACT II – Scene 1

Don Giovanni and Leporello stand before the balcony of Elvira's house.

Don Giovanni:
Eh via, buffone, non mi seccar!

Don Giovanni:
Come on buffoon, don't annoy me!

Leporello:
No, no, padrone, non vo'restar.

Leporello:
No, master, I want to leave you.

Don Giovanni:
Sentimi, amico.

Don Giovanni:
Listen to me, my friend.

Leporello:
Vo'andar, vi dico!

Leporello:
I tell you that I'm leaving!

Don Giovanni:
Ma che ti ho fatto che vuoi lasciarmi?

Don Giovanni:
What have I done that makes you want to leave me?

Leporello:
O niente affatto!
Quasi ammazzarmi!

Leporello:
Of course nothing important!
It's just that you almost had me killed!

Don Giovanni:
Va, che sei matto, fu per burlar

Don Giovanni:
Go away. You're crazy. It was a joke.

Leporello:
Ed io non burlo, ma voglio andar!

Leporello:
I'm not joking, I want to leave you!

Don Giovanni:
Leporello!

Don Giovanni:
(Don Giovanni tries to detain Leporello)
Leporello!

Leporello:
Signore!

Leporello:
Sir!

Don Giovanni:
Vien qui, facciamo pace, prendi!

Don Giovanni: *(gives him a purse)*
Here, let's make peace. Take this!

Leporello:
Cosa?

Leporello:
How much?

Don Giovanni::
Quattro doppie.

Don Giovanni:
Four gold pieces.

Leporello:
Oh, sentite: per questa volta la ceremonia accetto; ma non vi ci avvezzate;
non credete di sedurre i miei pari, come le donne, a forza di danari.

Leporello: *(counting the money)*
O.K. Listen, I'll accept it just this once, but don't make it a habit. Don't think that you can seduce me with the power of money the way you do the women.

Don Giovanni:
Non parliam più di ciò!
Ti basta l'animo di far quel ch'io ti dico?

Don Giovanni:
Let's not talk about it anymore!
Do you have the courage to do what I'm about to tell you?

Leporello:
Purchè lasciam le donne.

Leporello:
Provided we give up women.

Don Giovanni:
Lasciar le donne? Pazzo!
Sai ch'elle per me son necessarie più del pan che mangio,
più dell'aria che spiro!

Don Giovanni:
Give up women? You're mad!
You know that they're more necessary to me than the bread I eat, or the air I breathe!

Leporello:
E avete core d'ingannarle poi tutte?

Leporello:
And why do you have the heart to deceive all of them?

Don Giovanni:
È tutto amore! Chi a una sola è fedele, verso l'altre è crudele:
io che in me sento sì esteso sentimento,
vo' bene a tutte quante.
Le donne poiché calcolar non sanno,
il mio buon natural chiamano inganno.

Don Giovanni:
It is all for love! A man who is faithful to one, is cruel to all the others.
I, who has within me such immense feelings, I want to love them all.
But, the women misinterpret my good intentions and consider them deceptions.

Leporello:
Non ho veduto mai naturale più vasto, e più benigno.
Orsù, cosa vorreste?

Leporello:
I have never seen such grand benevolence, and such a good nature.
Now, what do you want me to do?

Don Giovanni:
Odi! Vedesti tu la cameriera di Donna Elvira?

Don Giovanni:
Listen! Have you seen Donna Elvira's maid?

Leporello:
Io? No!

Leporello:
Me? No!

Don Giovanni:
Non hai veduto qualche cosa di bello, caro il mio Leporello;
ora io con lei vo' tentar la mia sorte, ed ho pensato, giacché siam verso sera, per

Don Giovanni:
Then my dear Leporello, you have missed something lovely. Right now, I'm going to try my luck with her, and I've been thinking, since it's almost evening,

aguzzarle meglio l'appetito di presentarmi a lei col tuo vestito.

I'll arouse her appetite by presenting myself in your clothes.

Leporello:
E perchè non potreste presentarvi col vostro?

Leporello:
And why can't you present yourself in your own clothes?

Don Giovanni:
Han poco credito con genti di tal rango gli abiti signorili.

Don Giovanni:
With people like her, the dress of a noble would appear too fine.

Sbrigati, via!

(Don Giovanni takes off his cloak)
Be quick!

Leporello:
Signor, per più ragioni…

Leporello:
Sir, I've a suspicion….

Don Giovanni:
Finiscila! Non soffro opposizioni!

Don Giovanni:
Stop it! I can't stand opposition!

Don Giovanni and Leporello exchange cloaks and hats.

Donna Elvira:
Ah taci, ingiusto core!
Non palpitarmi in seno!
È un empio, e un traditore.
È colpa di aver pietà.

Donna Elvira: *(from her balcony)*
Be silent, inconsiderate heart!
Don't throb in my breast!
He's merciless, and he's a deceiver.
It's shameful to have pity for him.

Leporello:
(Zitto! Di Donna Elvira, Signor, la voce io sento!)

Leporello:
(Sssh! I hear Donna Elvira's voice!)

Don Giovanni:
(Cogliere io vo' il momento, tu fermati un po' là!)

Don Giovanni:
(I'll seize the opportunity! You stand over there!)

Don Giovanni stands behind Leporello and makes gestures with Leporello's arms.

Elvira, idolo mio!

Elvira, my idol!

Donna Elvira:
Non è costui l'ingrato?

Donna Elvira:
Is that the ingrate?

Don Giovanni:
Si, vita mia, son io, e chieggo carità.

Don Giovanni:
Yes, my dearest, it is I, and I ask for your forgiveness.

Donna Elvira:
(Numi, che strano affetto, mi si risveglia in petto!)

Donna Elvira:
(Gods, what strange emotion he arouses in my breast!)

Leporello:
(State a veder la pazza, che ancor gli crederà!)

Leporello:
(Look at that crazy woman! She still believes him!)

Don Giovanni:
Discendi, o gioia bella, vedrai che tu sei quella che adora l'alma mia pentito io sono già.

Don Giovanni:
Come down, my beautiful jewel, and you'll see that you are the one who my soul adores. I have already repented.

Donna Elvira:
No, non ti credo, o barbaro!

Donna Elvira:
I don't believe you, you barbarian!

Don Giovanni:
Ah credimi, o m'uccido!
Idolo mio, vien qua!

Don Giovanni:
Believe me, or I'll kill myself!
My idol, come here!

Leporello:
(Se seguitate, io rido!)

Leporello:
(If you continue, I'll burst out laughing!)

Donna Elvira:
(Dei, che cimento è questo!
Non so s'io vado o resto!
Ah proteggete voi la mia credulità!)

Donna Elvira:
(Gods, what agony this is!
I don't know whether to go or remain!
Gods, protect me from my uncertainty!)

Don Giovanni:
(Spero che cada presto!
Che bel colpetto è questo!
Più fertile talento del mio, no, non si dà!)

Don Giovanni:
(I think it worked well!
What an ingenious stroke this was!
A more fertile talent than mine doesn't exist!)

Leporello:
(Già quel mendace labbro torna a sedur costei, deh proteggete, o dei!
La sua credulità!)

Leporello:
(What a smooth deceiver he is!
I hope the gods protect her from her uncertainty!)

Elvira leaves the balcony

Don Giovanni:
Amore, che ti par?

Don Giovanni: *(happily)*
What do you think?

Leporello:
Mi par che abbiate un'anima di bronzo.

Leporello:
I think that you are heartless.

Don Giovanni:
Va là, che sei il gran gonzo!
Ascolta bene: quando costei qui viene, tu corri ad abbracciarla, falle quattro carezze, fingi la voce mia: poi con bell'arte cerca teco condurla in altra parte.

Don Giovanni:
So be it. What a fool you are!
Now listen to me. When she comes out, run and embrace her, give her four kisses, and mimic my voice. Then use your ingenuity and take her somewhere else.

Leporello:
Ma, Signor...

Leporello:
But, sir…

Don Giovanni:
Non più repliche!

Don Giovanni:
No more talk!

Leporello:
Ma se poi mi conosce?

Leporello:
But what if she recognizes me?

Don Giovanni:
Non ti conoscerà, se tu non vuoi.
Zitto: ell'apre, ehi giudizio!

Don Giovanni:
She won't recognize you, if you don't want her to.
Quiet! She's opening the door, so be smart!

Don Giovanni rushes off to the side, leaving Leporello alone.
Donna Elvira emerges from the house, and advances toward Leporello.

Donna Elvira:
Eccomi a voi.

Donna Elvira: *(to Leporello)*
I am here for you.

Don Giovanni:
(Veggiamo che farà.)

Don Giovanni: *(to Leporello)*
(Let's see what will happen.)

Leporello:
(Che bell'imbroglio!)

Leporello:
(What a beautiful predicament!)

Donna Elvira:
Dunque creder potrò che i pianti miei abbian vinto quel cor?
Dunque pentito l'amato Don Giovanni al suo dovere all'amor mio ritorna?

Donna Elvira:
Could I ever have believed that my tears have won your heart?
Has my beloved Don Giovanni repented, and returned to me virtuous and faithful?

Leporello:
Sì, carina!

Leporello: *(imitating Don Giovanni's voice)*
Yes, beloved!

Donna Elvira:
Crudele! Se sapeste quante lagrime e quanti sospir voi mi costaste!

Donna Elvira:
You cruel man! If you only knew much I cried and longed for you!

Leporello:
Io, vita mia?

Leporello:
My beloved, for me?

Donna Elvira:
Voi.

Leporello:
Poverina! Quanto mi dispiace!

Donna Elvira:
Mi fuggirete più?

Leporello:
No, muso bello!

Donna Elvira:
Sarete sempre mio?

Leporello:
Sempre!

Donna Elvira:
Carissimo!

Leporello:
Carissima!
(La burla mi dà gusto.)

Donna Elvira:
Mio tesoro!

Leporello:
Mia Venere!

Donna Elvira:
Son per voi tutta foco.

Leporello:
Io tutto cenere.

Don Giovanni:
(Il birbo si riscalda.)

Donna Elvira:
E non m'ingannerete?

Leporello:
No, sicuro.

Donna Elvira:
Giuratelo.

Donna Elvira:
Yes, for you.

Leporello:
Poor lady! I'm so sorry for you!

Donna Elvira:
Will you ever leave me again?

Leporello:
No, my beautiful inspiration!

Donna Elvira:
Will you always be mine?

Leporello:
Always!

Donna Elvira:
My dearest!

Leporello:
My dearest!
(I'm really enjoying this game.)

Donna Elvira:
My treasure!

Leporello:
My Venus!

Donna Elvira: *(embracing him)*
I'm all aflame for you.

Leporello:
And I am all burned to ashes.

Don Giovanni:
(The rogue is warming up to it.)

Donna Elvira:
Will you ever deceive me again?

Leporello:
Certainly not.

Donna Elvira:
Swear it.

Leporello:
Lo giuro a questa mano, che bacio con trasporto, e a que' bei lumi.

Leporello:
I swear it by this hand, my kiss for you, and on your beautiful eyes.

Don Giovanni:
Ah, eh, ah, ah!
Sei morto.

Don Giovanni:
(pretending to thrash someone)
Ah, ha, you wretch, you're dead!

Donna Elvira e Leporello:
Oh numi!

Donna Elvira and Leporello:
Oh, heavens!

In fear, Donna Elvira and Leporello flee together.

Don Giovanni:
Ha, ha, ha! Par che la sorte mi secondi; veggiamo! Le finestre son queste. Ora cantiamo.

Don Giovanni:
Ha, ha, ha! It seems that luck is with me! Let's see! These are the windows. Now, we'll sing the serenade.

Don Giovanni serenades Donna Elvira's maid, accompanying himself with the mandolin Leporello left behind.

Deh, vieni alla finestra, o mio tesoro,
deh, vieni a consolar il pianto mio.
Se neghi a me di dar qualche ristoro,
davanti agli occhi tuoi morir vogl'io!

Tu ch'hai la bocca dolce più del miele,
Tu che il zucchero porti in mezzo al core!
Non esser, gioia mia, con me crudele!
Lasciati almen veder, mio bell'amore!

Come to the window, my treasure.
Come and console my tears.
If you refuse to give me some solace, I wish to die before your eyes!

Your mouth is sweeter than honey!
You carry sweetness in your heart!
My treasure, don't be cruel to me!
My beautiful love let me at least see you!

Don Giovanni:
V'è gente alla finestra,
forse è dessa! Sst! Sst!

Don Giovanni:
There's someone at the window.
Perhaps it is she! Psst! Psst!

Masetto arrives, armed with a gun and pistol. Peasants follow him.

Masetto:
Non ci stanchiamo;
il cor mi dice che trovarlo dobbiam.

Masetto: *(to the peasants)*
Let's never give up. My intuition tells me that we should find him here.

Don Giovanni:
(Qualcuno parla!)

Don Giovanni:
(Someone is speaking!)

Masetto:
Fermatevi; mi pare che alcuno qui si muova.

Masetto: *(to the peasants)*
Stop here! It seems to me that someone moved.

Don Giovanni:

(Se non fallo, è Masetto!)

Don Giovanni:
(hiding himself with his cloak and hat)
(If I'm not mistaken, it's Masetto!)

Masetto:
Chi va là? Non risponde; animo, schioppo al muso! Chi va là?

Masetto;
Who's there? No one answers.
Be courageous friends, and have your muskets ready! Who's there?

Don Giovanni:
(Non è solo, ci vuol giudizio.)

Amici. (Non mi voglio scoprir.)
Sei tu, Masetto?

Don Giovanni:
(He's not alone. I better be careful.)
(imitating Leporello)
Friends. (I don't want them to recognize me.)
Masetto, is that you?

Masetto:
Appunto quello; e tu?

Masetto:
Precisely, and you?

Don Giovanni:
Non mi conosci? Il servo son io di Don Giovanni.

Don Giovanni:
Don't you recognize me? I'm Don Giovanni's servant.

Masetto:
Leporello! Servo di quell'indegno cavaliere!

Masetto:
Leporello! The servant of that disreputable cavalier!

Don Giovanni:
Certo; di quel briccone!

Don Giovanni:
That's right, the servant of that rascal!

Masetto:
Di quell'uom senza onore: ah, dimmi un poco dove possiam trovarlo? Lo cerco con costor per trucidarlo!

Masetto;
Of that dishonorable man. Tell me, where we can find him? We're all looking to slaughter him!

Don Giovanni:
(Bagattelle!) Bravissimo, Masetto!
Anch'io con voi m'unisco, per fargliela a quel birbo di padrone.
Ma udite un po' qual è la mia intenzione.

Metà di voi qua vadano,
e gli altri vadan là!
E pian pianin lo cerchino.
Lontan non fia di qua!

Don Giovanni:
(So that's all!) Great, Masetto!
I'll join you to help you catch my wicked master. But listen a moment to what I have in mind.

Half of you go this way,
and the rest go that way!
And we'll look for him very quietly.
He can't be far from here!

Se un uom e una ragazza
passeggian per la piazza,
se sotto a una finestra
fare all'amor sentite,
ferite pur, ferrite!
Il mio padron sarà!

If you should see a man and a lady
walk through the square,
or if you hear someone
making love under a window,
then wound him!
It will be my master.

In testa egli ha un cappello
con candidi pennacchi.
Addosso un gran mantello,
e spada al fianco egli ha.
Andate, fate presto!

He wears a hat on his head
that has white plumes.
There's a large cloak on his shoulder,
and a sword at his side.
Go on, go quickly!

Don Giovanni pushes the peasants away to pursue their prey.

Don Giovanni:
Tu sol verrai con me. Noi far dobbiamo il resto, e già vedrai cos'è!

Don Giovanni: *(to Masetto)*
But you come with me! We can do the rest ourselves, and you'll soon see what that is!

Zitto, lascia ch'io senta! Ottimamente: dunque dobbiam ucciderlo?

Quiet, let me listen! Perfect. So why do you want to kill him?

Masetto:
Sicuro!

Masetto:
Certainly!

Don Giovanni:
E non ti basterìa rompergli l'ossa, fracassargli le spalle?

Don Giovanni:
Wouldn't it be enough to break his bones and fracture his back?

Masetto:
No, no, voglio ammazzarlo, vo' farlo in cento brani.

Masetto:
No, I want to kill him! I want to tear him into a hundred pieces.

Don Giovanni:
Hai buone armi?

Don Giovanni:
Do you have good weapons?

Masetto:
Cospetto! Ho pria questo moschetto, e poi questa pistola.

Masetto:
Of course! I have this musket, and then this pistol.

Masetto hands the musket and pistol to Don Giovanni.

Don Giovanni:
E poi?

Don Giovanni:
And what else?

Masetto:
Non basta?

Masetto:
Isn't that enough?

Don Giovanni beats Masetto with the flat part of his sword.

Don Giovanni:
Eh, basta certo. Or prendi: questa per la pistola, questa per il moschetto.

Don Giovanni:
Certainly enough. Now, take this for the pistol, and this for the musket.

Masetto:
Ahi, ahi! La testa mia!

Masetto: *(crying as he falls to the ground)*
Ay, ay! My head!

Don Giovanni:
Taci, o t'uccido!
Questi per ammazzarlo, questi per farlo in brani!
Villano, mascalzon! Ceffo da cani!

Don Giovanni:
Quiet, or you'll get killed!
This is for wanting to kill him, and this for wanting to tear him apart!
Villain, bumpkin! Ugly dog!

Don Giovanni throws the weapons down before Masetto, and then leaves hastily.

Masetto:
Ahi! Ahi! La testa mia! Ahi, ahi! Le spalle e il petto!

Masetto: *(crying loudly)*
Ay! Ay! My head! Ay, ay! My back! My chest!

Zerlina:
Di sentire mi parve la voce di Masetto!

Zerlina: *(approaching with a lantern)*
I thought I just heard Masetto's voice!

Masetto:
O Dio, Zerlina mia, soccorso!

Masetto:
Oh god, Zerlina, help me!

Zerlina:
Cosa è stato?

Zerlina:
What happened?

Masetto:
L'iniquo, il scellerato i ruppe l'ossa e i nervi.

Masetto:
That villain and scoundrel broke all my bones.

Zerlina:
Oh poveretta me! Chi?

Zerlina:
Oh dear!! Who?

Masetto:
Leporello! Qualche diavol che somiglia a lui!

Masetto:
Leporello! Or else some devil who resembles him!

Zerlina:
Crudel! Non te diss'io che con questa tua pazza gelosia ti ridurresti a qualche brutto passo?
Dove ti duole?

Zerlina: *(helping Masetto to rise)*
How cruel! Didn't I tell you that your senseless jealousy would get you into trouble?
Where does it hurt you?

Masetto:
Qui.

Masetto:
Here.

Zerlina:
E poi?

Zerlina:
Where else?

Masetto:
Qui, e ancora qui!

Masetto:
Here, and also here!

Zerlina:
E poi non ti duol altro?

Zerlina:
And are you hurt anywhere else?

Masetto:
Duolmi un poco questo pie', questo braccio, e questa mano.

Masetto:
I have some pain in this foot, this arm, and this hand.

Zerlina:
Via, via, non è gran mal, se il resto è sano. Vientene meco a casa; purché tu mi prometta d'essere men geloso, io, io ti guarirò, caro il mio sposo.

Zerlina:
Oh well, it's not so bad. It'll be back to health with a little rest. Come home with me. But now you must promise me not to be so jealous.

Vedrai, carino,
se sei buonino,
che bel rimedio
ti voglio dar!

You'll see, my love.
I'll cure you.
You'll see, dearest, if you are good,
I'll give you a beautiful remedy!

È naturale,
non dà disgusto,
e lo speziale
non lo sa far.

It's natural,
not offensive,
and the herbalist
doesn't make it.

È un certo balsamo
ch'io porto addosso,
dare tel posso,
se il vuoi provar.

It's a certain balm
that I carry with me.
If you want to try it
I can give it to you.

Saper vorresti dove mi sta?
Sentilo battere, toccami qua!

Would you like to know where I keep it? Feel it beating, touch me here!

Zerlina places Masetto's hand on her heart, and then both leave.

ACT II – Scene 2

A dark courtyard before Donna Anna's house. There are three doors. Leporello, wearing Don Giovanni's hat and cloak, appears with Donna Elvira.

Leporello:
Di molte faci il lume s'avvicina, o mio ben: stiamo qui un poco finché da noi si scosta.

Leporello:
Lots of torchlights are approaching. My love, let's stay here awhile until they pass by..

Donna Elvira:
Ma che temi, adorato mio sposo?

Donna Elvira:
What are you so afraid of, my adored husband?

Leporello:
Nulla, nulla. Certi riguardi, io vo' veder se il lume è già lontano.
(Ah, come da costei liberarmi?)
Rimanti, anima bella!

Leporello:
Nothing, nothing. I just want to see if the torchlights are far away.
(How can I free myself from her?)
My love, wait here a moment!

Donna Elvira:
Ah! Non lasciarmi! Sola, sola in buio loco palpitar il cor mi sento, e m'assale un tal spavento, che mi sembra di morir.

Donna Elvira:
(as Leporello moves further away)
Oh, don't leave me! Alone, alone here in this dark place, I feel my heart throbbing. And I'm overcome by such fear, that I feel like I'm going to die.

Leporello:
(Più che cerco, men ritrovo questa porta sciagurata;
Piano, piano, l'ho trovata!
Ecco il tempo di fuggir!)

Leporello: *(groping his way around)*
(The more I search the more difficult to find that infernal door.
Easy, easy! I've found it!
Now is the time to escape from her!)

In the dark, Leporello finds a door, but then misses it again.

Don Octavio and Donna Anna arrive; she is dressed in mourning clothes.

Don Ottavio:
Tergi il ciglio, o vita mia, e dà calma a tuo dolore! L'ombra omai del genitore pena avrà de' tuoi martir.

Don Octavio:
Dry those tears, my love and calm your grieving! The spirit of your father will be upset by your agonizing.

Donna Anna:
Lascia almen alla mia pena questo piccolo ristoro; sol la morte, o mio tesoro, il mio pianto può finir.

Donna Anna:
At least there is some consolation in my sorrow. It is only death, my love, that can end my tears.

Donna Elvira:
Ah dov'è lo sposo mio?

Donna Elvira: *(unseen by the others)*
Oh, where is my husband?

Leporello:
(Se mi trova, son perduto!)

Leporello: *(by the door, also unseen)*
(If she finds me, I'm finished!)

Donna Elvira:
Una porta là vegg'io,

Donna Elvira: *(approaches the door)*
I see a door there.

Leporello:
Cheto, cheto, vo'partir!

Leporello:
Quietly, quietly, here's my chance to leave!

At the door, Leporello is confronted by Masetto and Zerlina.

All surround Leporello, who kneels and hides his face in his cloak.

Zerlina e Masetto:
Ferma, briccone, dove ten vai?

Zerlina and Masetto:
Stop, scoundrel! Where are you going?

Donna Anna e Don Ottavio:
Ecco il fellone! Com'era qua?

Donna Anna and Don Octavio:
Here's the criminal! Why is he here?

Donna Anna, Zerlina, Don Ottavio, Masetto:
Ah, mora il perfido che m'ha tradito!

Donna Anna Zerlina, Don Octavio, Masetto:
Death to this perfidious scoundrel!

Donna Elvira:
È mio marito! Pietà!

Donna Elvira: *(unveils herself)*
He is my husband! Have mercy on him!

Donna Anna, Zerlina, Don Ottavio, Masetto:
È Donna Elvira? Quella ch'io vedo? Appena il credo!
No, no, morrà!

Donna Anna Zerlina, Don Octavio, Masetto:
Is that Donna Elvira? Is that who I see?
I can't believe it!
No, no, death to him!

Leporello:
Perdon, perdono, signori miei! Quello io non sono, sbaglia costei! Viver lasciatemi per carità!

Leporello: *(as if crying)*
Forgive me, my lords! She is mistaken. I am not that man! For Heaven's sake, let me live!

All are astonished as Leporello reveals his identity.

Donna Anna, Zerlina, Don Ottavio, Masetto:
Dei! Leporello! Che inganno è questo!
Stupido resto! Che mai sarà?

Donna Anna Zerlina, Don Octavio, Masetto:
Gods! Leporello! What a deception this is! I'm astonished! How can this be?

Leporello:
(Mille torbidi pensieri mi s'aggiran per la testa; se mi salvo in tal tempesta, è un prodigio in verità.)

Leporello:
(A thousand turbulent thoughts are spinning in my head. If I escape from such a storm, it will be a true miracle.)

Donna Anna leaves. Leporello tries unsuccessfully to follow.

Donna Anna, Zerlina, Don Ottavio, Masetto:
(Mille torbidi pensieri Mi s'aggiran per la testa:
Che giornata, o stelle, è questa!
Che impensata novità!)

Donna Anna Zerlina, Don Octavio, Masetto:
(A thousand turbulent thoughts are spinning in my head.
Oh heavens, what a day this has become! What an unexpected event!)

Zerlina:
Dunque quello sei tu, che il mio Masetto poco fa crudelmente maltrattasti!

Zerlina: *(furiously to Leporello)*
So it was you, who only a short while ago cruelly maltreated Masetto!

Donna Elvira:
Dunque tu m'ingannasti, o scellerato, spacciandoti con me per Don Giovanni!

Donna Elvira: *(to Leporello)*
So it was you who wickedly deceived me, you rogue, by imitating Don Giovanni!

Don Ottavio:
Dunque tu in questi panni venisti qui per qualche tradimento!

Don Octavio:
So it was you who came here in that disguise to deceive us!

Donna Elvira:
A me tocca punirlo.

Donna Elvira:
Let me punish him.

Zerlina:
Anzi a me.

Zerlina:
Let me do it.

Don Ottavio:
No, no, a me.

Don Octavio:
No, no, let me.

Masetto:
Accoppatelo meco tutti e tre.

Masetto:
Let's all three of us deal with him.

Leporello:
Ah, pietà, signori miei!
Dò ragione a voi, a lei
ma il delitto mio non è.
Il padron con prepotenza,
l'innocenza mi rubò.

Leporello:
Have mercy, my lords!
You are right, and so is she.
But I'm not the guilty one.
My tyrannical master
robbed me of my innocence.

Donna Elvira, compatite!
Voi capite come andò!

(to Donna Elvira)
Donna Elvira, be compassionate!
You understand that he made me do it!

Di Masetto non so nulla,
vel dirà questa fanciulla.

(to Masetto and pointing to Donna Elvira)
This girl will tell you,
that I know nothing about Masetto.

È un oretta circumcirca,
che con lei girando vo.

I was going around with her
for an hour or so.

A voi, signore, non dico niente,
certo timore, certo accidente,
di fuori chiaro, di dentro scuro,
non c'è riparo, la porta, il muro.

(to Don Octavio)
To you, sir, I say nothing.
Certain fears and certain mishaps
are overtly clear, but obscure inside.
There is no hiding place, the door, the wall

Io me ne vado verso quel lato, poi qui celato,
l'affar si sa!
Ma s'io sapeva, fuggìa per qua!

(slyly moving toward the door)
I'll go that way, toward the side, and
then hide there.
But if I only knew how to escape from here!

Leporello runs out quickly.

Donna Elvira:
Ferma, perfido, ferma!

Donna Elvira:
Stop scoundrel! Stop!

Masetto:
Il birbo ha l'ali ai piedi!

Masetto:
The rascal has wings on his feet!

Zerlina:
Con qual arte si sottrasse l'iniquo.

Zerlina:
He got out of here so skillfully.

Don Ottavio:
Amici miei, dopo eccessi sì enormi,
dubitar non possiam che
Don Giovanni non sia l'empio uccisore del
padre di Donn'Anna;
in questa casa per poche ore fermatevi, un
ricorso vo'far a chi si deve, e in pochi istanti
vendicarvi prometto.

Don Octavio:
My friends, after such enormous
offences, we can no longer doubt that
Don Giovanni was the merciless
murderer of Donna Anna's father.
Stay here for a few hours. I'll have
recourse to justice, and I promise that
you will have vengeance very soon.

Così vuole dover, pietade, affetto!

Duty demands it, compassion, and affection!

Donna Elvira, Zerlina and Masetto leave.

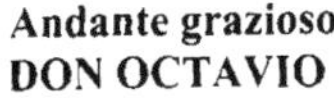

Il mio tesoro intanto andate a consolar,
e del bel ciglio il pianto cercate di asciugar.

Meanwhile, my dearest treasure, console
yourself, and wipe away the tears from
your beautiful eyes.

Ditele che i suoi tortia cendicar io vado;
Che sol di stragi e morti nunzio vogl'io
tornar.

I am going to have vengeance against those
who wronged her. I will only return only
when I can announce that we have been
avenged by carnage and death.

Zerlina, with a razor in her hand, drags Leporello in.

Zerlina: Restati qua!	**Zerlina:** You stay here!
Leporello: Per carità, Zerlina!	**Leporello:** *(trying to free himself)* Zerlina, for heaven's sake!
Zerlina: Eh! Non c'è carità pei pari tuoi.	**Zerlina:** There's no mercy for what you're going to suffer.
Leporello: Dunque cavar mi vuoi?	**Leporello:** Do you want to bury me?
Zerlina: I capelli, la testa, il cor e gli occhi!	**Zerlina:** I'll cut the hair on your head, and gouge out your eyes!
Leporello: Senti, carina mia!	**Leporello:** *(trying to dissuade her)* Listen, my dear!
Zerlina: Guai se mi tocchi! Vedrai, schiuma de' birbi, qual premio n'ha chi le ragazze ingiuria.	**Zerlina:** *(repelling him)* Careful not to touch me! You'll see, you rogue, what gift you'll get from an injured girl.
Leporello: (Liberatemi, o Dei, da questa furia!)	**Leporello:** (Gods, free me from this woman's fury!)
Zerlina: Masetto, olà, Masetto! Dove diavolo è ito? Servi! Gente! Nessun vien, nessun sente.	**Zerlina:** Masetto, Masetto! Where the devil has he gone? Servants! People! No one comes, no one hears.
Leporello: Fa piano, per pietà! Non trascinarmi a coda di cavallo!	**Leporello:** *(a peasant enters)* Easy, for heaven's sake! Don't drag me like a sack of grain!
Zerlina: Vedrai, vedrai come finisce il ballo! Presto qua quella sedia!	**Zerlina:** You'll see that I haven't even started! Quickly, here in this seat!
Leporello: Eccola!	**Leporello:** Here!
Zerlina: Siedi!	**Zerlina:** Sit!

Leporello:
Stanco non son.

Leporello:
I'm not tired.

Zerlina:
Siedi, o con queste mani ti strappo il cor e poi lo getto ai cani.

Zerlina:
Sit, or with these I'll tie you up and throw you to the dogs.

Leporello:
Siedo, ma tu, di grazia, metti giù quel rasoio mi vuoi forse sbarbar?

Leporello: *(sits down)*
I'm seated, but for Heaven's sake, put down that razor. Do you want to shave me?

Zerlina:
Sì, mascalzone! Io sbarbare ti vo' senza sapone.

Zerlina:
Yes, you rascal! I want to shave you without soap.

Leporello:
Eterni Dei!

Leporello:
Eternal gods!

Zerlina:
Dammi la man!

Zerlina:
Give me your hand!

Leporello:
La mano?

Leporello:
My hand?

Zerlina:
L'altra!

Zerlina:
Now the other one!

Leporello:
Ma che vuoi farmi?

Leporello:
What do you want to do with me?

Zerlina:
Voglio far, voglio far quello che parmi!

Zerlina:
I want to do; I want to do what pleases me!

Zerlina ties Leporello's hands, assisted by the peasant.

Leporello:
Per queste tue manine candide e tenerelle, per questa fresca pelle, abbi pietà di me!

Leporello:
Have pity on me! Have mercy on these two white and tender hands and this soft skin!

Zerlina:
Non v'è pietà, briccone;
son una tigre irata, un aspide, un leone.
No, no, non v'è pietà!

Zerlina:
There is no pity, rogue. I am an inflamed tiger, an asp, and a lion. No, no, there is no mercy for you!

Leporello:
Ah! Di fuggir si provi!

Leporello:
Oh! If I could only try to escape!

Zerlina:
Sei morto se ti movi!

Zerlina:
Your dead if you move!

Leporello:
Barbari, ingiusti Dei!
In mano di costei chi capitar mi fe'?

Leporello:
Barbarian, unjust gods! Who would believe that my fate is in your hands?

Zerlina:
Barbaro traditore! Del tuo padrone il core avessi qui con te!

Zerlina: *(ties Leporello to the chair)*
Barbarous traitor! You too have your master's evil heart!

Leporello:
Deh! Non mi stringer tanto, l'anima mia sen va!

Leporello:
Heh! Don't tie me so tight!

Zerlina:
Sen vada o resti, intanto non partirai di qua!

Zerlina:
Faint or relax, but you won't get away from here!

Leporello:
Che strette, o Dei, che botte!
E giorno, ovver è notte?
Che scosse di tremuoto!
Che buia oscurità!

Leporello:
So tight, oh gods, what a disaster!
Is it day or is it night?
What shaking and quivering!
What a gloomy execution!

Zerlina:
Di gioia e di diletto sento brillarmi il petto.
Così, così, cogli uomini, così, così si fa!

Zerlina:
I feel sparkles of joy and delight in my breast. This is the only way to treat men!

Zerlina departs. Leporello is tied in the chair. In desperation, he asks help from the peasant.

Leporello:
Amico, per pietà, un poco d'acqua fresca o ch'io mi moro!
Guarda un po' come stretto mi legò l'assassina!

Leporello:
Friend, for mercy's sake, a little fresh water or I'll die!
Look how tightly that assassin tied me!

After the peasant departs, Leporello struggles to free himself.

Se potessi liberarmi coi denti?
Oh, venga il diavolo a disfar questi gruppi!

Io vo' veder di rompere la corda come è forte!
Paura della morte!
E tu, Mercurio, protettor de' ladri,
proteggi un galantuomo coraggio!

Could I free myself by using my teeth?
Or, maybe the devil will come to cut these cords!
Let me see how strong the cord is, and if I can break it!
I fear that I'm going to die
And you, Mercury, protector of robbers,
assist a gallant and courageous man!

Leporello pulls hard. The window, to which the cord was fastened, falls.

Bravo! Pria che costei ritorni bisogna dar di sprone alle calcagna, e trascinar, se occorre una montagna.

Great! Before they return, I'll need spurs on my heels to run and cross the mountain.

Leporello escapes, dragging the chair and window with him.

Zerlina enters, with Donna Elvira, Masetto and peasants.

Zerlina:
Andiam, andiam, Signora! Vedrete in qual maniera ho concio il scellerato.

Zerlina:
Madam! Let's go and see how I punished the scoundrel.

Donna Elvira:
Ah! Sopra lui si sfoghi il mio furore!

Donna Elvira:
Oh! You have vented my fury on him!

Zerlina:
Stelle! In qual modo si salvò il briccone?

Zerlina:
Heavens! How could the scoundrel have escaped?

Donna Elvira:
L'avrà sottratto l'empio suo padrone.

Donna Elvira:
He has stolen the villainy of his master.

Zerlina:
Fu desso senza fallo: anche di questo informiam Don Ottavio; a lui si spetta far per noi tutti, o domandar vendetta!

Zerlina:
You're absolutely right! We must inform Don Octavio about this. He wants to exact revenge for all of us.

Masetto and the peasants leave.

Donna Elvira:
In quali eccessi, o Numi, in quai misfatti orribili, tremendi è avvolto il sciagurato!
Ah no! Non puote tardar l'ira del cielo, la giustizia tardar.
Sentir già parmi la fatale saetta, che gli piomba sul capo!
Aperto veggio il baratro mortal!
Misera Elvira!
Che contrasto d'affetti, in sen ti nasce!
Perchè questi sospiri?
E queste ambascie?

Donna Elvira:
Oh gods, this wretch is involved in such horrible and tremendous excesses!
Oh no! Heaven's anger cannot be delayed, or justice postponed!
I already feel the fatal thunderbolt falling on his head!
I see the deadly abyss open!
Poor Elvira!
What conflicting emotions have emerged in your heart! Why these sighs?
Why this anguish?

Allegro assai
DONNA ELVIRA

Mi tradì, quell'alma ingrata, infelice, o Dio, mi fa.
Ma tradita e abbandonata, provo ancor per lui pietà.

Oh god, that ungrateful soul betrayed me and has made me unhappy.
But even though he betrayed and abandoned me, I still feel pity for him.

Quando sento il mio tormento, di vendetta il cor favella, ma se guardo il suo cimento, palpitando il cor mi va.

When I feel my anguish, my heart cries in jeopardy, my heart starts throbbing for him.

ACT II - Scene 3

A walled cemetery with several statues, among them, a statue of the Commandant. Don Giovanni leaps over the wall, still wearing Leporello's hat.

Don Giovanni:
Ah, ah, ah, questa è buona, or lasciala cercar; che bella notte!
È più chiara del giorno, sembra fatta per gir a zonzo a caccia di ragazze.

È tardi? Oh, ancor non sono due della notte; Avrei voglia un po'di saper come è finito l'affar tra Leporello e Donna Elvira, s'egli ha avuto giudizio!

Don Giovanni: *(laughing)*
Ha, ha, ha, this is good. Now let her try to find me!
What a beautiful night! It's brighter than the day; and seems to urge me to rove about and hunt for pretty girls.
Is it late? Oh, it's not yet two in the morning. I would really like to know how things went with Leporello and Donna Elvira, and if he was successful with her!

Leporello:
Alfin vuole ch'io faccia un precipizio.

Leporello: *(from behind the wall)*
Surely, he wishes to ruin me!

Don Giovanni:
(È desso.) Oh, Leporello!

Don Giovanni:
(That's him.) Oh, Leporello!

Leporello:
Chi mi chiama?

Leporello:
Who's calling me?

Don Giovanni:
Non conosci il padron?

Don Giovanni:
Don't you recognize your master?

Leporello:
Così non conoscessi!

Leporello:
I wish I never knew him!

Don Giovanni:
Come, birbo?

Don Giovanni:
What did you say, you rogue?

Leporello:
Ah, siete voi? Scusate!

Leporello:
Oh, is that you? Excuse me!

Don Giovanni:
Cosa è stato?

Don Giovanni:
What happened?

Leporello:
Per cagion vostra io fui quasi accoppato.

Leporello:
Because of you, I was almost killed.

Don Giovanni:
Ebben, non era questo un onore per te?

Don Giovanni:
Well, wasn't that an honor for you?

Leporello:
Signor, vel dono.

Leporello:
Sir, you can have the honor.

Don Giovanni:
Via, via, vien qua! Che belle cose ti deggio dir.

Don Giovanni:
Come, come this way! I've some great things to tell you!

Leporello:
Ma cosa fate qui?

Leporello:
But what are you doing here?

Don Giovanni:
Vien dentro e lo saprai. Diverse storielle che accadute mi son da che partisti, ti dirò un'altra volta: or la più bella ti vo'solo narrar.

Don Giovanni:
Come inside and you'll find out. Several things happened to me since you were away. I'll tell you another time, but the best one I'll tell you now.

Leporello climbs over the wall and exchanges hat and cloak with Don Giovanni.

Leporello:
Donnesca al certo?

Leporello:
Is it about women?

Don Giovanni:
C'è dubbio? Una fanciulla, bella, giovin, galante, per la strada incontrai; le vado appresso, la prendo per la man, fuggir mi vuole; dico poche parole, ella mi piglia, sai per chi?

Don Giovanni:
Do you doubt it? I met a charming and beautiful young girl while I was on the road. I approached her, but when I took her hand, she tried to run away. After a few words she took me for. Whom do you think?

Leporello:
Non lo so.

Leporello:
I don't know.

Don Giovanni:
Per Leporello!

Don Giovanni:
For Leporello!

Leporello:
Per me?

Leporello:
For me?

Don Giovanni:
Per te.

Don Giovanni:
For you.

Leporello:
Va bene.

Leporello:
Good.

Don Giovanni:
Per la mano essa allora mi prende.

Don Giovanni:
Then she took me by the hand.

Leporello:
Ancora meglio.

Leporello:
Even better.

Don Giovanni:
M'accarezza, mi abbraccia:
"Caro il mio Leporello! Leporello, mio caro!"
Allor m'accorsi ch'era qualche tua bella.

Don Giovanni:
She kissed me, she embraced me: "My dearest Leporello! Leporello, my dear!" Then I realized that she was one of your girls.

Leporello:
(Oh maledetto!)

Leporello:
(Damn it!)

Don Giovanni:
Dell'inganno approfitto; non so come mi riconosce, grida; sento gente, a fuggire mi metto, e pronto pronto per quel muretto in questo loco io monto.

Don Giovanni:
I took advantage of it. Unfortunately, somehow she recognized me and began to shout. People approached and then it was time to run away. So quick as light, I jumped here over this wall.

Leporello:
E mi dite la cosa con tanta indifferenza?

Leporello:
And why do you tell this to me so casually?

Don Giovanni:
Perché no?

Don Giovanni:
Why not?

Leporello:
Ma se fosse costei stata mia moglie?

Leporello:
But what if that pretty girl was my wife?

Don Giovanni:
Meglio ancora!

Don Giovanni: *(laughing loudly)*
Even better!

The moon breaks through the clouds, casting light on the Statue of the Commandant. Then the Statue speaks.

La Statua:
Di rider finirai pria dell'aurora!

The Statue:
Your laughter will end before dawn!

Don Giovanni:
Chi ha parlato?

Don Giovanni:
Who spoke?

Leporello:
Ah! Qualche anima sarà dell'altro mondo, che vi conosce a fondo.

Leporello: *(in extreme fear)*
Oh, some ghost from another world, who recognizes you well.

Don Giovanni:
Taci, sciocco! Chi va là?

Don Giovanni:
(striking some statues with his sword)
Quiet, you fool! Who goes there?

La Statua:
Ribaldo, audace! Lascia a' morti la pace!

The Statue:
Insolent rogue! Let the dead sleep in peace!

Leporello:
Ve l'ho detto!

Leporello: *(trembling)*
I told you!

Don Giovanni:
Sarà qualcun di fuori che si burla di noi!

Don Giovanni:
It's someone outside playing a joke on us!

Ehi, del Commendatore non è questa la statua? Leggi un poco quella iscrizion.

(with indifference and contempt)
Hey, isn't that the statue of the Commandant? Read me the inscription.

Leporello:
Scusate. Non ho imparato a leggere ai raggi della luna.

Leporello:
Excuse me: I never learned to read by moonlight.

Don Giovanni:
Leggi, dico!

Don Giovanni:
(grasps his sword to threaten Leporello)
Read it!

Leporello:
"Dell'empio che mi trasse al passo estremo qui attendo la vendetta."
Udiste? Io tremo!

Leporello: *(reads the inscription)*
"Here, I await vengeance upon the evil man who ended my life."
Did you hear that? I'm trembling!

Don Giovanni:
O vecchio buffonissimo! Digli che questa sera l'attendo a cenar meco!

Don Giovanni:
You old buffoon! Tell him that I expect him to join me for dinner tonight!

Leporello:
Che pazzia ! Ma vi par, oh Dei, mirate, che terribili occhiate egli ci dà! Par vivo! Par che senta, e che voglia parlar!

Leporello:
What madness! I won't. Oh heavens, look at how sternly he glares at us! He seems alive! He seems to hear! He wants to speak!

Don Giovanni:
Orsù, va là! O qui t'ammazzo, e poi ti seppellisco!

Don Giovanni:
Go on! Or I'll kill you, and then bury you!

Leporello:
Piano, piano, signore, ora ubbidisco.
O statua gentilissima del gran Commendatore.
Padron! Mi trema il core, non posso terminar!

Leporello:
Master, easy, easy. As you please.
Oh, most illustrious statue of the great Commandant. Master! My heart is trembling, I can't go on!

Don Giovanni:
Finiscila, o nel petto ti metto questo acciar!

Don Giovanni:
Finish it, or I'll put this steel through your heart!

Leporello:
(Che impiccio, che capriccio!)

Leporello:
(What a mess! What a caprice!)

Don Giovanni:
(Che gusto! Che spassetto!)

Don Giovanni:
(What fun! What amusement!)

Leporello:
Io sentomi gelar!

Leporello:
I feel a chill!

Don Giovanni:
Lo voglio far tremar!

Don Giovanni:
I want to make him tremble!

Leporello:
O statua gentillissima, benchè di marmo siate. Ah padron mio! Mirate! Che seguita a guardar!

Leporello:
Oh, most illustrious statue, even though you are of marble. Master! Look! His eyes are glowing!

Don Giovanni:
Mori!

Don Giovanni:
(advances menacingly toward the Statue)
Die!

Leporello:
No, no, attendete! Signor, il padron mio, badate ben, non io, vorria con voi cenar! Ah che scena è questa!

Oh ciel! Chinò la testa!

Leporello:
No, wait! *(to the Statue)* My lord, my master, not I, would like to dine with you! What a scene this is!
(the Statue nods in approval)
Oh heavens! He nodded his head!

Don Giovanni:
Va là, che sei un buffone!

Don Giovanni: *(not looking at the Statue)*
You're a buffoon!

Leporello:
Guardate ancor, padrone!

Leporello:
Master, look again!

Don Giovanni:
E che degg'io guardar?

Don Giovanni:
What should I look at?

Leporello:
Colla marmorea testa, ei fa così, così!

Leporello: *(imitating the statue)*
He goes like this with his marble head!

Don Giovanni e Leporello:
Colla marmorea testa, ei fa così, così!

Don Giovanni and Leporello:
(the statue bends its head)
He goes like this with his marble head!

Don Giovanni:
Parlate, se potete! Verrete a cena?

Don Giovanni: *(to the Statue)*
Speak if you can! Will you come to dinner?

La Statua:
Sì!

The Statue: *(inclining its head)*
Yes!

Leporello:
Mover mi posso, appena, mi manca, o Dei, la lena! Per carità, partiamo, partiamo via di qua! Andiamo via di qua!

Leporello:
I can hardly move. I have no strength. For mercy's sake, let's go! For heaven's sake, let's leave. Let's leave here! Let's go!

Don Giovanni:
Bizzarra è inver la scena, verrà il buon vecchio a cena a prepararla andiamo, partiamo via di qua!
Andiamo via di qua!

Don Giovanni:
The scene is indeed bizarre. The old man will come to dinner. Let's go and prepare dinner. Let's leave here!
Let's go!

ACT II – Scene 4

A room in Donna Anna's house.

Don Ottavio:
Calmatevi, idol mio! Di quel ribaldo vedrem puniti in breve i gravi eccessi, vendicati sarem.

Don Octavio:
Be calm, my love! Soon this libertine shall be punished for his grave excesses. We shall be avenged.

Donna Anna:
Ma il padre, o Dio!

Donna Anna:
Oh god, my poor father!

Don Ottavio:
Convien chinare il ciglio al volere del ciel. Respira, o cara! Di tua perdita amara fia doman, se vuoi, dolce compenso, questo cor, questa mano, che il mio tenero amor.

Don Octavio:
But we must bow our heads to the will of heaven. Rest my dear! For tomorrow your bitter loss will be sweetly rewarded by my tender love, my heart, and my hand.

Donna Anna:
O dei, che dite in sì tristi momenti?

Donna Anna:
What do you talk about at such sad moments?

Don Ottavio:
E che? Vorresti con indugi novelli accrescer le mie pene? Ah! Crudele!

Don Octavio:
What? Do you want to increase my pain with renewed postponements? Oh, you are so cruel!

Donna Anna:
Crudele? Ah no, giammai mio ben! Troppo mi spiace allontanarti un ben che lungamente la nostr'alma desia.
Ma il mondo, o Dio!

Non sedur la costanza del sensibil mio core; ahbastanza per te mi parla amore!

Donna Anna:
Cruel? Oh, no, my love! I regret so much that I must turn you away from a happiness our souls have long desired.
Oh god, it is this horrible world!

Do not tempt the faithfulness of my sensitive heart! It is enough for you that love speaks to me!

Larghetto
DONNA ANNA

Non mi dir, bell'idol mio, che son io crudel con te.

Don't tell me, my dear love, that I am cruel to you.

Tu ben sai quant'io t'amai, tu conosci la mia fè!
Calma, calma il tuo tormento, se di duol non vuoi ch'io mora! Forse un giorno il cielo ancora sentirà pietà di me!

You know well how much I have loved you, and you know my faith!
Calm your torment if you do not want me to die of sorrow! Perhaps one day, heaven will yet feel mercy for me!

(Donna Anna exits)

Don Ottavio:
Ah si segua il suo passo; io vo' con lei dividere i martiri.
Saran meco men gravi i suoi sospiri

Don Octavio:
Ah! Let me follow her footsteps. I'll share her grieving.
Her sorrows will be less if she shares them with me.

ACT II – Scene 5

A large illuminated hall. A sumptuous banquet has been prepared.

Don Giovanni:
Già la mensa è preparata. Voi suonate, amici cari!
Giacché spendo i miei danari, io mi voglio divertir. Leporello, questa tavola!

Don Giovanni:
The table is already prepared. Play music, dear friends!
Since I'm spending my money, I want to enjoy myself. Leporello, serve!

Leporello:
Son prontissimo a servir.

Leporello:
Sir, I'm ready to serve.

The musicians play a melody from Martin's "Una cosa rara."

Leporello:
Bravi! "Cosa rara!"

Leporello:
Terrific! "Cosa rara!"

Don Giovanni:
Che ti par del bel concerto?

Don Giovanni:
How do you like the concert?

Leporello:
È conforme al vostro merto.

Leporello:
It's consistent with your excellence.

Don Giovanni:
Ah che piatto saporito!

Don Giovanni:
Such delicious food!

Leporello:
(Ah che barbaro appetito!
Che bocconi da gigante!
Mi par proprio di svenir!)

Leporello:
(Such a barbarous appetite!
What gigantic mouthfuls!
I think I'm going to faint from hunger!)

Don Giovanni:
(Nel veder i miei bocconi
gli par proprio di svenir.)
Piatto!

Don Giovanni:
(Watching my mouthfuls, I think he's
going to faint from hunger.)
Another plate here!

Leporello:
Servo.

Leporello:
I'll serve it to you.

The musicians begin to play Paisiello's "Fra I due litiganti il terzo gode."

Evvivano "I litiganti."

Cheers for "The litigants."

Don Giovanni:
Versa il vino! Eccellente marzimino!

Don Giovanni:
Pour more wine! Excellent red wine!

Leporello:
(Questo pezzo di fagiano, piano piano
vo'inghiottir.)

Leporello:
(I'll eat this piece of pheasant quietly.)

Don Giovanni:
(Sta mangiando, quel marrano! Fingerò di
non capir.)

Don Giovanni:
(That rascal is eating! I'll pretend not to
see.)

The musicians play music from Mozart's "The Marriage of Figaro."

Leporello:
Questa poi la conosco pur troppo.

Leporello:
I know this one too well.

Don Giovanni:
Leporello!

Don Giovanni: *(ignoring Leporello)*
Leporello!

Leporello:
Padron mio!

Leporello: *(with his mouth full)*
Yes, my master!

Don Giovanni:
Parla schietto, mascalzone.

Don Giovanni:
Speak more clearly, you rogue.

Leporello:
Non mi lascia una flussione le parole proferir.

Leporello: *(clearing his throat)*
My mouth is hoarse.

Don Giovanni:
Mentre io mangio fischia un poco.

Don Giovanni:
Whistle a little something while I'm eating.

Leporello:
Non so far.

Leporello:
I don't know how to whistle.

Don Giovanni:
Cos'è?

Don Giovanni: *(looking at Leporello)*
What's that you say?

Leporello:
Scusate! Sì eccellente è il vostro cuoco, che lo volli anch'io provar.

Leporello:
Excuse me! Your cook is so wonderful that I wanted to taste it too.

Don Giovanni:
(Sì eccellente è il cuoco mio, che lo volle anch'ei provar.)

Don Giovanni:
(Yes, my cook is so excellent, that he wanted to taste it too.)

Donna Elvira:
L'ultima prova dell'amor mio ancor vogl'io fare con te. Più non rammento gl'inganni tuoi, pietade io sento.

Donna Elvira: (*entering* *desperately)*
I want to make the last test of my love for you. I will forget your betrayals. I will be merciful to you.

Don Giovanni e Leporello:
Cos'è?

Don Giovanni and Leporello:
What is this?

Donna Elvira:

Da te non chiede quest'alma oppressa della sua fede qualche mercè.

Donna Elvira:
(kneeling before Don Giovanni)
This injured soul asks mercy from you.

Thunder is heard from an approaching storm.

Don Giovanni:
Mi maraviglio! Cosa volete?
Se non sorgete non resto in piè.

Don Giovanni: *(trying to raise her)*
I am amazed! What do you want?
If you don't rise, I'll kneel with you.

Donna Elvira:
Ah non deridere gli affani miei!

Donna Elvira:
Don't mock my anguish!

Leporello:
(Quasi da piangere mi fa costei.)

Leporello:
(She almost makes me cry.)

Don Giovanni:
Io te deridere? Cielo, e perché?
Che vuoi, mio bene?

Don Giovanni: *(raising Elvira tenderly)*
Would I mock you? Heavens, why?
What is it you want, my love?

Donna Elvira:
Che vita cangi!

Donna Elvira:
That you change your life!

Don Giovanni:
Brava!

Don Giovanni:
Excellent!

Donna Elvira:
Cor perfido!

Donna Elvira:
Faithless heart!

Don Giovanni:
Lascia ch'io mangi, e se ti piace, mangia con me.

Don Giovanni: *(sitting down at the table)*
Let me eat. And if you wish, join me.

Donna Elvira:
Rèstati, barbaro! Nel lezzo immondo esempio orribile d'iniquità!

Donna Elvira: *(disdainfully)*
Barbarian! Then remain in your indecent filth and dreadful wickedness!

Don Giovanni:
Vivan le femmine.
Viva il buon vino!
Sostegno e gloria d'umanità!

Don Giovanni: *(raising his glass)*
Here's to women!
Here's to good wine!
They are the nourishment and glory of humanity!

Leporello:
(Se non si muove al suo dolore, di sasso ha il core, o cor non ha.)

Leporello:
(She cannot move him with her suffering. His heart is of stone, or he has no heart.)

Donna Elvira rushes out to the door, and becomes terrified when she sees the Statue. Then she departs through another door.

Donna Elvira:
Ah!

Donna Elvira:
Ah!

Don Giovanni e Leporello:
Che grido è questo mai?

Don Giovanni and Leporello:
What was the reason for that scream?

Don Giovanni:
Va a veder che cosa è stato!

Don Giovanni:
Go and see what happened!

Leporello:
Ah!

Leporello: *(upon seeing the Statue)*
Ah!

Don Giovanni:
Che grido indiavolato!
Leporello, che cos'è?

Don Giovanni:
What a diabolic shout!
Leporello, what is it?

Leporello:
Ah, signor, per carità! Non andate fuor di qua! L'uom di sasso, l'uomo bianco. Ah padrone! Io gelo, io manco. Se vedeste che figura, se sentiste come fa ta ta ta ta!

Leporello: *(in fright)*
Ah, sir, for heaven's sake! Don't go out there! The man of stone, the man of marble. Master! I'm chilled, I'm fainting. If you saw that figure. If you hear his ta ta ta ta!

Don Giovanni:
Non capisco niente affatto. Tu sei matto in verità.

Don Giovanni:
I don't understand it at all. You're indeed mad.

There is knocking on the door.

Leporello:
Ah sentite!

Leporello:
Listen!

Don Giovanni:
Qualcun batte! Apri!

Don Giovanni:
Someone's knocking! Open it!

Leporello:
Io tremo!

Leporello:
I'm trembling!

Don Giovanni:
Apri, dico!

Don Giovanni:
Open the door!

Leporello:
Ah!

Leporello:
No!

Don Giovanni:
Matto! Per togliermi d'intrico ad aprir io stesso andrò.

Don Giovanni:
Idiot! To solve this puzzle I'll go and open it myself.

Leporello:
(Non vo' più veder l'amico pian pianin m'asconderò.)

Leporello:
(I'll never see our friend again. I'll quietly hide.)

Don Giovanni opens the door. Leporello hides under the table. Amid a clap of thunder, the Statue of the Commandant appears.

La Statua:
Don Giovanni, a cenar teco m'invitasti e son venuto!

The Statue:
Don Giovanni, you invited me to dine with you, and I have come!

Don Giovanni:
Non l'avrei giammai creduto; ma farò quel che potrò. Leporello, un altra cena fa che subito si porti!

Don Giovanni:
I would never have believed it, but I'll do what I can. Leporello, another dinner. Have it brought immediately!

Leporello:
Ah padron! Siam tutti morti!

Leporello: *(peeking from under the table)*
Oh master! We're all going to die!

Don Giovanni:
Vanne dico!

Don Giovanni:
Listen to me!

La Statua:
Ferma un po'! Non si pasce di cibo mortale chi si pasce di cibo celeste; altra cure più gravi di queste, altra brama quaggiù mi guidò!

The Statue:
Stop a moment! No nourishment from mortal food for one who is nourished by celestial food. I am guided here by other cares and cravings that are more solemn than these!

Leporello:
(La terzana d'avere mi sembra e le membra fermar più non sò.)

Leporello:
(It's like having a fever. My limbs won't stop shaking.)

Don Giovanni:
Parla dunque! Che chiedi!
Che vuoi?

Don Giovanni:
Then speak! What do you ask for?
What do you want?

La Statua:
Parlo; ascolta! Più tempo non ho!

The Statue:
I'll speak and you listen! I have little time!

Don Giovanni:
Parla, parla, ascoltando ti sto.

Don Giovanni: *(angrily and defiantly)*
Then speak. I am listening to you.

La Statua:
Tu m'invitasti a cena, il tuo dover or sai.
Rispondimi: verrai tu a cenar meco?

The Statue:
You invited me to dinner. You now know your duty. Answer me: will you come to dine with me?

Leporello:
Oibò; tempo non ha, scusate.

Leporello: *(trembling from far away)*
Make an excuse. Tell him you have no time now.

Don Giovanni:
A torto di viltate tacciato mai sarò!

Don Giovanni: *(calmly and coldly)*
I shall never be accused of cowardice!

La Statua:
Risolvi!

The Statue: *(impatiently)*
Then decide!

Don Giovanni:
Ho già risolto!

Don Giovanni:
I have decided!

La Statua:
Verrai?

The Statue:
Will you come?

Leporello:
Dite di no!

Leporello: *(to Don Giovanni)*
Say no!

Don Giovanni:
Ho fermo il cuore in petto: non ho timor: verrò!

Don Giovanni:
My heart is beating steadily. I'm not afraid. I'll come!

La Statua:
Dammi la mano in pegno!

The Statue: *(offering his left hand)*
Give me your hand as a pledge!

Don Giovanni:
Eccola! Ohimé!

Don Giovanni: *(offering his right hand)*
Here it is! Let go!

La Statua:
Cos'hai?

The Statue:
What is it?

Don Giovanni:
Che gelo è questo mai?

Don Giovanni:
What is this deadly coldness?

La Statua:
Pentiti, cangia vita.
È l'ultimo momento!

The Statue:
Repent and change your life!
This is your last chance!

Don Giovanni:
No, no, ch'io non mi pento. Vanne lontan da me!

Don Giovanni: *(vainly tries to free himself)*
No, no, I won't repent! Get far away from me!

La Statua:
Pentiti, scellerato!

The Statue:
Repent, you scoundrel!

Don Giovanni:
No, vecchio infatuato!

Don Giovanni:
No, old fool!

La Statua:
Pentiti!

The Statue:
Repent!

Don Giovanni:
No!

Don Giovanni:
No!

La Statua:
Sì!

The Statue:
Yes!

Don Giovanni:
No!

Don Giovanni:
No!

La Statua:
Ah! Tempo più non v'è!

The Statue:
There is no more time!

As the Statue disappears, the earth trembles, and flames rise from all sides.

Don Giovanni:
Da qual tremore insolito sento assalir gli spiriti! Dond'escono quei vortici di foco pien d'orror?

Don Giovanni:
What strange fears! I feel the spirits assailing me! Where have those whirlpools of fire and terror come from?

Coro di diavoli:
Tutto a tue colpe è poco!
Vieni, c'è un mal peggior!

Chorus of Devils: *(from below)*
It is too little punishment for your sins!
Come, there is even worse for you!

Don Giovanni:
Chi l'anima mi lacera!
Chi m'agita le viscere!
Che strazio, ohimé, che smania!
Che inferno, che terror!

Don Giovanni:
They rip my soul!
They agitate my insides!
What torture, what delirium!
What hell! What terror!

Leporello:
(Che ceffo disperato! Che gesti da dannato!
Che gridi, che lamenti! Come mi fa terror!)

Leporello:
(What desperate cries! What noise from the damned! What shouts, what laments! How if fills me with terror!)

Don Giovanni:
Ah!

Don Giovanni: *(the flames engulf him)*
Ah!

Leporello:
Ah!

Leporello:
Ah!

ACT II – Scene 6

Donna Anna, Donna Elvira, Zerlina, Don Octavio and Masetto, accompanied by ministers of justice.

Donna Elvira, Zerlina, Don Ottavio e Masetto:
Ah, dov'è il perfido?
Dov'è l'indegno?
Tutto il mio sdegno sfogar io vo'!

Donna Elvira, Zerlina, Don Octavio and Masetto:
Where is that perfidious man?
Where is that contemptible man?
I want to unleash all of my anger!

Donna Anna:
Solo mirandolo stretto in catene alle mie pene calma darò.

Donna Anna:
My pain can only be calmed if I see him bound in chains.

Leporello:
Più non sperate di ritrovarlo, più non cercate. Lontano andò.

Leporello: *(pale and trembling)*
Don't expect to see him again. Search no more. He's gone far away.

Tutti:
Cos'è? Favella! Via presto, sbrigati!

All:
What is it? Tell us! Hurry up!

Leporello:
Venne un colosso.

Leporello:
A gigantic statue came.

Tutti:
Via presto, sbrigati!

All:
Tell us! Hurry up!

Leporello:
Ma se non posso. Tra fumo e fuoco. Badate un poco. L'uomo di sasso... Fermate il passo. Giusto là sotto, diede il gran botto. Giusto là il diavolo. Sel trangugiò!

Leporello:
But I can't go on. Listen a moment. It was amidst smoke and fire. The man of stone... He seized him. Just there in the ground, he gave the great blow. The devil swallowed him up and he vanished!

Tutti:
Stelle, che sento!

All:
Heavens, what do I hear!

Leporello:
Vero è l'evento!

Leporello:
It's all quite true!

Donna Elvira:
Ah, certo è l'ombra che m'incontrò.

Donna Elvira:
It must have been the ghost I met.

Donna Anna, Zerlina, Don Ottavio e Masetto:
Ah, certo è l'ombra che l'incontrò.

Donna Anna, Zerlina, Don Octavio and Masetto:
It must have been the ghost she met.

Don Ottavio:
Or che tutti, o mio tesoro, vendicati siam dal cielo. Porgi, porgi a me un ristoro, non mi far languire ancor.

Don Octavio: *(to Donna Anna)*
My treasure, now that all of us are vindicated by heaven, console me, and don't let me languish any more.

Donna Anna:
Lascia, o caro, un anno ancora allo sfogo del mio cor.

Donna Anna:
My dear, let another year pass for my grief to run its course.

Don Ottavio:
Al desio di chi m'adora ceder deve un fido amor.

Don Octavio:
A faithful love must submit to the desires of one who adores him.

Donna Anna:
Al desio di chi t'adora ceder deve un fido amor.

Donna Anna: *(offers Octavio her hand)*
A faithful love must submit to the desires of one whom he loves.

Donna Elvira:
Io men vado in un ritiro a finir la vita mia!

Donna Elvira:
(to Donna Anna and Don Octavio)
I'll go into a convent for the rest of my life!

Zerlina:
Noi, Masetto, a casa andiamo! A cenar in compagnia!

Zerlina:
Masetto, let's go home and dine together!

Masetto:
Noi, Zerlina, a casa andiamo! A cenar in compagnia!

Masetto:
Zerlina, let's go home and dine together!

Leporello:
Ed io vado all'osteria a trovar padron miglior.

Leporello:
And I'm going to the inn to find a better master.

Zerlina, Masetto e Leporello:
Resti dunque quel birboncon Proserpina e Pluton.
E noi tutti, o buona gente, ripetiam allegramente l'antichissima canzon.

Zerlina, Masetto and Leporello:
Let the scoundrel remain with Persephene and Pluto.
And now good people, let's all repeat the old, old song again.

Tutti:
Questo è il fin di chi fa mal; e de' perfidi la morte alla vita è sempre ugual.

All:
This is how all evildoers end. All the wicked die as they have lived.

END OF OPERA

Discography

1936 Brownlee (Giovanni); Souez (Anna); Helletsgrüber (Elvira); von Pataky (Octavio); Baccaloni (Leporello); Henderson (Masetto); Mildmay (Zerlina); Franklin (Commandant); Glundebourne Festival Chorus and Orchestra; Busch (Conductor)

1942 Pinza (Giovanni); Bampton (Anna); Novotna (Elvira); Kullmann (Octavio); Kipnis (Leporello); Harrell (Masetto); Sayáo (Zerlina); Cordon (Commandant); Metropolitan Opera Chorus and Orchestra (live performance); Walter (Conductor)

1943 (in German) Ahlersmayer (Giovanni); Schech (Anna); Teschemacher (Elvira); Hopf (Octavio); Böhme (Leporello); Frick (Masetto); Weidlich (Zerlina); Pflanzl (Commandant); Dresden State Opera Chorus/Saxon State Orchestra; Elmendorff (Conductor)

1950 (Live performance Salzburg Festival) Gobbi (Giovanni); Welitsch (Anna); Schwartzkopf (Elvira); Dermota (Octavio); Kunz (Leporello); Poell (Masetto); Seefried (Zerlina); Greindl (Commandant); Vienna State Opera Chorus/Vienna Philharmonic Orchestra; Furtwängler (Conductor)

1950 Stabile (Giovanni); Grob-Prandl (Anna); H. Konetzni (Elvira); Handt (Octavio); Pernerstorfer (Leporello); Poell (Masetto); Heusser (Zerlina); Czerwenka (Commandant); Vienna State Opera Chorus and Orchestra; Swarowsky (Conductor)

1953 Taddei (Giovanni); Curtis-Verna (Anna); Gavazzi (Elvira); Valletti (Octavio); Tajo (Leporello); Susca (Masetto); Ribetti (Zerlina); Zerbini (Commandant); Turin Radio Chorus and Orchestra; Rudolf (Conductor)

1954 (Live performance Salzburg Festival) Siepi (Giovanni); Grümmer (Anna); Schwarzkopf (Elvira); Dermota (Octavio); Edelmann (Leporello); Berry (Masetto); Berger (Zerlina); Ernster (Commandant); Vienna State Opera Chorus and Orchestra; Furtwängler (Conductor)

1955 London (Giovanni); Zadek (Anna); Jurinac (Elvira); Simoneau (Octavio); Berry (Leporello); Wächter (Masetto); Sciutti (Zerlina); Weber (Commandant); Vienna State Opera Chorus and Orchestra; Moralt (Conductor)

1955 Siepi (Giovanni); Danco (Anna); Della Casa (Elvira); Dermota (Octavio); Corena (Leporello); Berry (Masetto); Gueden (Zerlina) Böhme (Commandant); Vienna State Opera Chorus and Orchestra; Krips (Conductor)

1956 Campo (Giovanni); Stich-Randall (Anna); Danco (Elvira); Gedda (Octavio); Cortis (Leporello); Vessières (Masetto); Moffo (Zerlina); Arié (Commandant); Aix-en-Provence Festival Chorus/Paris Conservatoire Orchestra; Rosbaud (Conductor)

1958 Fischer-Dieskau (Giovanni); Jurinac (Anna); Stader (Elvira); Haefliger (Octavio); Kohn (Leporello); Sardi (Masetto); Seefried (Zerlina); Kreppel (Commandant); Berlina Radio Chorus and Symphony Orchestra; Fricsay (Conductor)

1958 Colombo (Giovanni); Kingdon (Anna); Graf (Elvira); Giraudeau (Octavio); Ollendorf (Leporello); Gorin (Masetto); Dobbs (Zerlina); Hofmann (Commandant); Netherlands State Opera Chorus and Orchestra; Krannhals (Conductor)

1959 Siepi (Giovanni); Nilsson (Anna); Price (Elvira); Valetti (Octavio); Corena (Leporello); Blankenburg (Masetto); Ratti (Zerlina); van Mill (Commandant); Vienna State Opera Chorus and Orchestra; Leinsdorf (Conductor)

1959 Wächter (Giovanni); Sutherland (Anna); Schwarzkopf (Elvira); Alva (Octavio); Taddei (Leporello); Cappuccilli (Masetto); Sciutti (Zerlina); Frick (Commandant); Philharmonia Chorus and Orchestra; Giulini (Conductor)

1965 Ghiaurov (Giovanni); Watson (Anna); Ludwig (Elvira); Gedda (Octavio); Berry (Leporello); Montarsolo (Masetto); Freni (Zerlina); Crass (Commandant); New Philharmonia Chorus and Orchestra; Klemperer (Conductor)

1966 Fischer-Dieskau (Giovanni); Nilsson (Anna); Arroyo (Elvira); Schreier (Octavio); Flagello (Leporello); Mariotti (Masetto); Grist (Zerlina); Talvela (Commandant); Prague National Theatre Chorus and Orchestra; Böhm (Conductor)

1969 Bacquier (Giovanni); Sutherland (Anna); Lorengar (Elvira); Krenn (Octavio); Gramm (Leporello); Monreale (Masetto); Horne (Zerlina); Grant (Commandant); Ambrosian Opera Chorus/English Chamber Orchestra; Bonynge (Conductor)

1973 Wixell (Giovanni); Arroyo (Anna); Te Kanawa (Elvira); Burrows (Octavio); Ganzarolli (Leporello); Van Allan (Masetto); Freni (Zerlina); Roni (Commandant); Royal Opera House Chorus and Orchestra; Davis (Conductor)

1973 Soyer (Giovanni); Sgourda (Anna); Harper (Elvira); Alva (Octavio); Evans (Leporello); Rinaldi (Masetto); Donath (Zerlina); Lagger (Commandant); Scottish Opera Chorus/English Chamber Orchestra; Barenboim (Conductor)

1977 (Live performance Salzburg Festival)
Milnes (Giovanni); Tomowa-Sintow (Anna); Zylis-Gara (Elvira); Schrier (Octavio); Berry (Leporello); Duesing (Masetto); Mathis (Zerlina); Macurdy (Commandant); Vienna State Opera Chorus/Salzburg Mozarteum Orchestra;
Böhm (Conductor)

1978 Raimondi (Giovanni); Moser (Anna); Te Kanawa (Elvira); Riegel (Octavio); van Dam (Leporello); King (Masetto); Berganza (Zerlina); Macurdy (Commandant); Paris Opéra Chorus and Orchestra; Maazel (Conductor)

1978 Weikl (Giovanni); M. Price (Anna); Sass (Elvira); Burrows (Octavio);
Bacquier (Leporello) Sramek (Masetto); Popp (Zerlina); Moll (Commandant);
London Opera Chorus/London Philharmonic Orchestra; Solti (Conductor)

1984 Allen (Giovanni); Vaness (Anna); Ewing (Elvira); Lewis (Octavio);
Van Allan (Leporello); Rawnsley (Masetto); Gale (Zerlina); Kavrakos (Commandant);
Glyndebourne Chorus/London Philharmonic Orchestra; Haitink (Conductor)

1985 Titus (Giovanni); Varady (Anna); Augér (Elvira); Moser (Octavio);
Panerai (Leporello); Scholtzke (Masetto); Mathis (Zerlina); Rootering (Commandant);
Navarian Radio Chorus and Symphony Orchestra; Kubelik (Conductor)

1985 Ramey (Giovanni); Tomowa-Sintow (Anna); Baltsa (Elvira); Winbergh (Octavio);
Furlanetto (Leporello); Malta (Masetto); Battle (Zerlina); Burchaladze (Commandant);
Berlin Opera CHorus/Berlin Philharmonic Orchestra; von Karajan (Conductor)

1987 Allen (Giovanni); Gruberova (Anna); Murray (Elvira); Araiza (Octavio);
Desderi (Leporello); De Carolis (Masetto); Mentzer (Zerlina);
Teatro all Scala Orchestra and Chorus; Muti (Conductor)

1988 Hampson (Giovanni); Gruberova (Anna); Alexander (Elvira); Blochwitz (Octavio);
Polgár (Leporello); Scharinger (Masetto); Bonney (Zerlina); Holl (Commandant);
Netherlands Opera Chorus/Concertgebouw Orchestra; Harnoncourt (Conductor)

1990 Shimell (Giovanni); Studer (Anna); Vaness (Elvira); Lopardo (Octavio);
Ramey (Leporello); De Carolis (Masettto); Mentzer (Zerlina);
Rootering (Commandant);
Vienna State Opera CHorus/Vienna Philharmonic Orchestra; Muti (Conductor)

1990 Furlanetto (Giovanni); Cuberli (Anna); Meier (Elvira); Heilmann (Octavio);
Tomlinson (Leporello); Pertusi (Masetto); Rodgers (Zerlina); Salminen (Commandant);
RIAS Chamber Chorus/Berlin Philharmonic Orchestra; Barenboim (Conductor)

1990 Hagehârd (Giovanni); Augér (Anna); Jones (Elvira); Meel (Octavio);
Cachemaille (Leporello); Terfel (Masetto); Bonney (Zerlina);
Sigmundsson (Commandant);
Drottningholm Court Theater Chorus and Orchestra; Ostman (Conductor)

1990 Allen (Giovanni); Sweet (Anna); Mattila (Elvira); Araiza (Octavio);
Alaimo (Leporello); Otelli (Masetto); McLaughlin (Zerlina); Lloyd (Commandant);
Ambrosian Opera Chorus/Academy of St. Martin in the Fields Orchestra;
Mariner (Conductor)

1991 Ramey (Giovanni); Tomowa Sintow (Anna); Varady (Elvira); Winbergh (Octavio);
Furlanetto (Leoporello); Malta (Masetto); Battle (Zerlina);
Wiener Philharmonic; von Karajan (Conductor)

1995 Gilfry (Giovanni); Orgonasova (Anna); Margiono (Elvira); Prégardien (Octavio);
D'Arcangelo (Leporello);
English Baroque/Monteverdi Choir; Gardiner (Conductor)

1996 Skovhus (Giovanni); Brewer (Anna); Lott (Elvira); Hadley (Octavio);
Corbeth (Leporello); Chiummo (Masetto); Focile (Zerlina);
Scottish Chamber Orchestra; Mackerras (Conductor)

2000 Terfel (Giovanni); Fleming (Anna); Kringelborn (Elvira); Groves (Octavio);
Furlanetto (Leporello); Relyea (Masetto); Hong (Zerlina);
Metropolitan Opera Chorus and Orchestra; Levine (Conductor)

2001 Gilfry (Giovanni); Rey (Anna); Sacca (Octavio); Bartoli (Elvira);
Polgar (Leporello); Widmer (Masetto); Nikiteanu (Zerlina)
Salminen (Commendatore);
Zurich Opera; Harnoncourt (Conductor)

Videography

DG Video/DVD (1954)

Siepi (Giovanni); Grümmer (Anna); Della Casa (Elvira); Dermota (Octavio); Edelmann (Leporello); Berry (Masetto); Berger (Zerlina); Wiener Philharmonic; Furtwängler (Conductor)

SONY VHS (1990)

Ramey (Giovanni); Tomowa-Sintow (Anna); Varady (Elvira); Winbergh (Octavio); Furlanetto(Leporello); Malta (Masetto); Battle (Zerlina); Burchaladze (Commandant); Vienna State Opera Chorus/Vienna Philharmonic Orchestra; von Karajan (Conductor); Hampe (Director); Viller (Video Director)

VIRGIN VHS (1990)

Hagegârd (Giovanni); Döse (Anna); Nordin (Elvira); Winbergh (Octavio); Saedén (Leporello); Wallström (Masetto); Soldh (Zerlina); Rudgren (Commandant); Drottningholm Chorus and Orchestra; Ostman (Conductor); Järvefelt (Director); Olofsson (Video Director)

Art Haus Musik DVD (1991)

Allen (Giovanni); Gruberova (Anna); Murray (Elvira); Araiza (Octavio); Desderi (Leporello); de Carolis (Masetto); Mentzer (Zerlina); Koptchak (Commandant); La Scala Chorus and Orchestra; Muti (Conductor); Strehler (Director); Battistoni (Video Director)

AE VHS/DVD (1992)

Raimondi (Giovanni); Moser (Anna); Te Kanawa (Elvira); Riegel (Octavio); van Dam (Leporello); King (Masetto); Berganza (Zerlina); Macurdy (Commandant); Paris Opéra Chorus and Orchestra; Maazel (Conductor); Losey (Director)

Art Haus Music (2001)

Gilfry (Giovanni); Rey (Anna) Bartoli (Elvira); Sacca (Octavio); Polgar (Leporello); Widmer (Masetto); Nikiteanu (Zerlina) Zurich Opera; Harnoncourt (Conductor)

UNIVERSAL & VI DVD (2005)

E. Perry (Giovanni); Labelle (Anna); H. Perry (Leporello); Hunt-Lieberson (Elvira); Peter Sellars production; Wiener Symphoniker; Smith (Conductor)

TDK DVD (2005)

Alvarez (Giovanni); Pieczonka (Anna); Antonacci (Elvira); Kirchschlager (Zerlina); Vienna Staatsoper; Muti (Conductor)

Dictionary of Opera and Musical Terms

Accelerando - Play the music faster, but gradually.

Adagio - At slow or gliding tempo, not as slow as Largo, but not as fast as Andante.

Agitato - Restless or agitated.

Allegro - At a brisk or lively tempo, faster than Andante but not as fast as Presto.

Andante - A moderately slow, easy-going tempo.

Appoggiatura - An extra or embellishing note preceding a main melodic note or tone. Usually written as a note of smaller size, it shares the time value of the main note.

Arabesque - Flourishes or fancy patterns usually applying to vocal virtuosity.

Aria - A solo song usually structured in a formal pattern. Arias generally convey reflective and introspective thoughts rather than descriptive action.

Arietta - A shortened form of aria.

Arioso - A musical passage or composition having a mixture of free recitative and metrical song.

Arpeggio - Producing the tones of a chord in succession but not simultaneously.

Atonal - Music that is not anchored in traditional musical tonality; it uses the chromatic scale impartially, does not use the diatonic scale and has no keynote or tonal center.

Ballad Opera - 18th century English opera consisting of spoken dialogue and music derived from popular ballad and folksong sources. The most famous is *The Beggar's Opera* which was a satire of the Italian opera seria.

Bar - A vertical line across the stave that divides the music into units.

Baritone - A male singing voice ranging between the bass and tenor.

Baroque - A style of artistic expression prevalent in the 17th century that is marked generally by the use of complex forms, bold ornamentation, and florid decoration. The Baroque period extends from approximately 1600 to 1750 and includes the works of the original creators of modern opera, the Camerata, as well as the later works by Bach and Handel.

Bass - The lowest male voices, usually divided into categories such as:

> **Basso buffo** - A bass voice that specializes in comic roles like Dr. Bartolo in Rossini's *The Barber of Seville*.
>
> **Basso cantante** - A bass voice that demonstrates melodic singing quality rather than comic or tragic: King Philip in Verdi's *Don Carlos*.
>
> **Basso profundo** - the deepest, most profound, or most dramatic of bass voices: Sarastro in Mozart's *The Magic Flute*.

Bel canto - Literally "beautiful singing." It originated in Italian opera of the 17th and 18th centuries and stressed beautiful tones produced with ease, clarity, purity, evenness, together with an agile vocal technique and virtuosity. Bel canto flourished in the first half of the 19th century in the works of Rossini, Bellini, and Donizetti.

Cabaletta - Typically a lively bravura extension of an aria or duet that creates a climax. The term is derived from the Italian word "cavallo," or horse: it metaphorically describes a horse galloping to the finish line.

Cadenza - A flourish or brilliant part of an aria commonly inserted just before a finale.

Camerata - A gathering of Florentine writers and musicians between 1590 and 1600 who attempted to recreate what they believed was the ancient Greek theatrical synthesis of drama, music, and stage spectacle; their experimentation led to the creation of the early structural forms of modern opera.

Cantabile - An expression indication urging the singer to sing sweetly.

Cantata - A choral piece generally containing Scriptural narrative texts: Bach Cantatas.

Cantilena - A lyrical melodic line meant to be played or sung "cantabile," or with sweetness and expression.

Canzone - A short, lyrical operatic song usually containing no narrative association with the drama but rather simply reflecting the character's state of mind: Cherubino's "Voi che sapete" in Mozart's *The Marriage of Figaro*. Shorter versions are called canzonettas.

Castrato - A young male singer who was surgically castrated to retain his treble voice.

Cavatina - A short aria popular in the 18th century without the da capo repeat section.

Classical Period - The period between the Baroque and Romantic periods. The Classical period is generally considered to have begun with the birth of Mozart (1756) and ended with Beethoven's death (1830). Stylistically, the music of the period stressed clarity, precision, and rigid structural forms.

Coda - A trailer or tailpiece added on by the composer after the music's natural conclusion.

Coloratura - Literally colored: it refers to a soprano singing in the bel canto tradition with great agility, virtuosity, embellishments and ornamentation: Joan Sutherland singing in Donizetti's *Lucia di Lammermoor.*

Commedia dell'arte - A popular form of dramatic presentation originating in Renaissance Italy in which highly stylized characters were involved in comic plots involving mistaken identities and misunderstandings. The standard characters were Harlequin and Colombine: The "play within a play" in Leoncavallo's *I Pagliacci.*

Comprimario - A singer portraying secondary character roles such as confidantes, servants, and messengers.

Continuo - A bass part (as for a keyboard or stringed instrument) that was used especially in baroque ensemble music; it consists of a succession of bass notes with figures that indicate the required chords. Also called *figured bass, thoroughbass.*

Contralto - The lowest female voice derived from "contra" against, and "alto" voice, a voice between the tenor and mezzo-soprano.

Countertenor, or male alto vocal range - A high male voice generally singing within the female high soprano ranges.

Counterpoint - The combination of one or more independent melodies added into a single harmonic texture in which each retains its linear character: polyphony. The most sophisticated form of counterpoint is the fugue form in which up to 6 to 8 voices are combined, each providing a variation on the basic theme but each retaining its relation to the whole.

Crescendo - A gradual increase in the volume of a musical passage.

Da capo - Literally "from the top": repeat. Early 17th century da capo arias were in the form of A B A, the last A section repeating the first A section.

Deus ex machina - Literally "god out of a machine." A dramatic technique in which a person or thing appears or is introduced suddenly and unexpectedly; it provides a contrived solution to an apparently insoluble dramatic difficulty.

Diatonic - Relating to a major or minor musical scale that comprises intervals of five whole steps and two half steps.

Diminuendo - Gradually getting softer, the opposite of crescendo.

Dissonance - A mingling of discordant sounds that do not harmonize within the diatonic scale.

Diva - Literally a "goddess"; generally refers to a female opera star who either possesses, or pretends to possess, great rank.

Dominant - The fifth tone of the diatonic scale: in the key of C, the dominant is G.

Dramma giocoso - Literally meaning amusing, or lighthearted. Like tragicomedy it represents an opera whose story combines both serious and comic elements: Mozart's *Don Giovanni.*

Falsetto - Literally a lighter or "false" voice; an artificially produced high singing voice that extends above the range of the full voice.

Fioritura - Literally "flower"; a flowering ornamentation or embellishment of the vocal line within an aria.

Forte, Fortissimo - Forte (*f*) means loud: mezzo forte (*mf*) is fairly loud; fortissimo (*ff*) even louder, and additional *fff*'s indicate greater degrees of loudness.

Glissando - A rapid sliding up or down the scale.

Grand Opera - An opera in which there is no spoken dialogue and the entire text is set to music, frequently treating serious and dramatic subjects. Grand Opera flourished in France in the 19th century (Meyerbeer) and most notably by Verdi (Aida): the genre is epic in scale and combines spectacle, large choruses, scenery, and huge orchestras.

Heldentenor - A tenor with a powerful dramatic voice who possesses brilliant top notes and vocal stamina. Heldentenors are well suited to heroic (Wagnerian) roles: Lauritz Melchoir in Wagner's *Tristan und Isolde*.

Imbroglio - Literally "Intrigue"; an operatic scene with chaos and confusion and appropriate diverse melodies and rhythms.

Largo or larghetto - Largo indicates a very slow tempo; Larghetto is slightly faster than Largo.

Legato - Literally "tied"; therefore, successive tones that are connected smoothly. Opposing Legato would be Marcato (strongly accented and punctuated) and Staccato (short and aggressive).

Leitmotif - A short musical passage attached to a person, thing, feeling, or idea that provides associations when it recurs or is recalled.

Libretto - Literally "little book"; the text of an opera. On Broadway, the text of songs is called "lyrics" but the spoken text in the play is called the "book."

Lied - A German song; the plural is "lieder." Originally German art songs of the 19th century.

Light opera, or operetta - Operas that contain comic elements but light romantic plots: Johann Strauss's *Die Fledermaus.*

Maestro - From the Italian "master": a term of respect to conductors, composers, directors, and great musicians.

Melodrama - Words spoken over music. Melodrama appears in Beethoven's *Fidelio* but flourished during the late 19th century in the operas of Massenet (*Manon*). Melodrama should not be confused with melodrama when it describes a work that is characterized by extravagant theatricality and by the predominance of plot and physical action over characterization.

Mezza voce - Literally "medium voice," or singing with medium or half volume; it is generally intended as a vocal means to intensify emotion.

Mezzo-soprano - A woman's voice with a range between that of the soprano and contralto.

Molto - Very. Molto agitato means very agitated.

Obbligato - An elaborate accompaniment to a solo or principal melody that is usually played by a single instrument.

Octave - A musical interval embracing eight diatonic degrees: therefore, from C to C is an octave.

Opera - Literally "a work"; a dramatic or comic play combining music.

Opera buffa - Italian comic opera that flourished during the bel canto era. Buffo characters were usually basses singing patter songs: Dr. Bartolo in Rossini's *The Barber of Seville,* and Dr. Dulcamara in Donizetti's *The Elixir of Love.*

Opéra comique - A French opera characterized by spoken dialogue interspersed between the arias and ensemble numbers, as opposed to Grand Opera in which there is no spoken dialogue.

Operetta, or light opera - Operas that contain comic elements but tend to be more romantic: Strauss's *Die Fledermaus,* Offenbach's *La Périchole*, and Lehar's *The Merry Widow*. In operettas, there is usually much spoken dialogue, dancing, practical jokes, and mistaken identities.

Oratorio - A lengthy choral work, usually of a religious or philosophical nature and consisting chiefly of recitatives, arias, and choruses but in deference to its content, performed without action or scenery: Handel's *Messiah.*

Ornamentation - Extra embellishing notes—appoggiaturas, trills, roulades, or cadenzas—that enhance a melodic line.

Overture - The orchestral introduction to a musical dramatic work that frequently incorporates musical themes within the work.

Parlando - Literally "speaking"; the imitation of speech while singing, or singing that is almost speaking over the music. It is usually short and with minimal orchestral accompaniment.

Patter - Words rapidly and quickly delivered. Figaro's Largo in Rossini's *The Barber of Seville* is a patter song.

Pentatonic - A five-note scale, like the black notes within an octave on the piano.

Piano - Soft volume.

Pitch - The property of a musical tone that is determined by the frequency of the waves producing it.

Pizzicato - A passage played by plucking the strings instead of stroking the string with the bow.

Polyphony - Literally "many voices." A style of musical composition in which two or more independent melodies are juxtaposed in harmony; counterpoint.

Polytonal - The use of several tonal schemes simultaneously.

Portamento - A continuous gliding movement from one tone to another.

Prelude - An orchestral introduction to an act or the whole opera. An Overture can appear only at the beginning of an opera.

Presto, Prestissimo - Very fast and vigorous.

Prima Donna - The female star of an opera cast. Although the term was initially used to differentiate between the dramatic and vocal importance of a singer, today it generally describes the personality of a singer rather than her importance in the particular opera.

Prologue - A piece sung before the curtain goes up on the opera proper: Tonio's Prologue in Leoncavallo's *I Pagliacci.*

Quaver - An eighth note.

Range - The divisions of the voice: soprano, mezzo-soprano, contralto, tenor, baritone, and bass.

Recitative - A formal device that that advances the plot. It is usually a rhythmically free vocal style that imitates the natural inflections of speech; it represents the dialogue and narrative in operas and oratorios. Secco recitative is accompanied by harpsichord and sometimes with cello or continuo instruments and *accompagnato* indicates that the recitative is accompanied by the orchestra.

Ritornello - A short recurrent instrumental passage between elements of a vocal composition.

Romanza - A solo song that is usually sentimental; it is usually shorter and less complex than an aria and rarely deals with terror, rage, and anger.

Romantic Period - The period generally beginning with the raiding of the Bastille (1789) and the last revolutions and uprisings in Europe (1848). Romanticists generally found inspiration in nature and man. Beethoven's *Fidelio* (1805) is considered the first Romantic opera, followed by the works of Verdi and Wagner.

Roulade - A florid vocal embellishment sung to one syllable.

Rubato - Literally "robbed"; it is a fluctuation of tempo within a musical phrase, often against a rhythmically steady accompaniment.

Secco - The accompaniment for recitative played by the harpsichord and sometimes continuo instruments.

Semitone - A half-step, the smallest distance between two notes. In the key of C, the notes are E and F, and B and C.

Serial music - Music based on a series of tones in a chosen pattern without regard for traditional tonality.

Sforzando - Sudden loudness and force; it must stick out from the texture and provide a shock.

Singspiel - Early German musical drama employing spoken dialogue between songs: Mozart's *The Magic Flute*.

Soprano - The highest range of the female voice ranging from lyric (light and graceful quality) to dramatic (fuller and heavier in tone).

Sotto voce - Literally "below the voice"; sung softly between a whisper and a quiet conversational tone.

Soubrette - A soprano who sings supporting roles in comic opera: Adele in Strauss's *Die Fledermaus*, or Despina in Mozart's *Così fan tutte.*

Spinto - From the Italian "spingere" (to push); a soprano having lyric vocal qualities who "pushes" the voice to achieve heavier dramatic qualities.

Sprechstimme - Literally "speak voice." The singer half sings a note and half speaks; the declamation sounds like speaking but the duration of pitch makes it seem almost like singing.

Staccato - Short, clipped, rapid articulation; the opposite of the caressing effects of legato.

Stretto - A concluding passage performed in a quicker tempo to create a musical climax.

Strophe - Music repeated for each verse of an aria.

Syncopation - Shifting the beat forward or back from its usual place in the bar; it is a temporary displacement of the regular metrical accent in music caused typically by stressing the weak beat.

Supernumerary - A "super"; a performer with a non-singing role: "Spear-carrier."

Tempo - Time, or speed. The ranges are Largo for very slow to Presto for very fast.

Tenor - Highest natural male voice.

Tessitura - The general range of a melody or voice part; but specifically, the part of the register in which most of the tones of a melody or voice part lie.

Tonality - The organization of all the tones and harmonies of a piece of music in relation to a tonic (the first tone of its scale).

Tone Poem - An orchestral piece with a program; a script.

Tonic - The keynote of the key in which a piece is written. C is the tonic of C major.

Trill - Two adjacent notes rapidly and repeatedly alternated.

Tutti - All together.

Twelve tone - The 12 chromatic tones of the octave placed in a chosen fixed order and constituting with some permitted permutations and derivations the melodic and harmonic material of a serial musical piece. Each note of the chromatic scale is used as part of the melody before any other note gets repeated.

Verismo - Literally "truth"; the artistic use of contemporary everyday material in preference to the heroic or legendary in opera. A movement from the late 19th century: *Carmen.*

Vibrato - A "vibration"; a slightly tremulous effect imparted to vocal or instrumental tone for added warmth and expressiveness by slight and rapid variations in pitch.

Made in the USA
Lexington, KY
19 April 2011